Real-Life
Discipleship

Made for Success Publishing
P.O. Box 1775 Issaquah, WA 98027
www.MadeForSuccessPublishing.com

Copyright © 2019 Tom Cheshire and Tom Gensler. All rights reserved.

In accordance with the U.S. Copyright Act of 1976, the scanning, uploading, and electronic sharing of any part of this book without the permission of the publisher constitutes unlawful piracy and theft of the author's intellectual property. If you would like to use material from the book (other than for review purposes), prior written permission must be obtained by contacting the publisher at service@madeforsuccess.net.

All Scriptures are taken from THE HOLY BIBLE, ENGLISH STANDARD VERSION (ESV): ® Copyright© 2001 by Crossway, a publishing ministry of Good News Publishers. Used by permission.

Thank you for your support of the author's rights.

Made for Grace is an imprint of Made for Success Publishing.

First Printing

Library of Congress Cataloging-in-Publication data
Cheshire, Tom and Gensler, Tom
    Real-Life Discipleship: The Ordinary Man's Guide to Disciple-Making
    p. cm.

ISBN: 978-1-64146-443-7(PBK)
ISBN: 978-1-64146-444-4 (eBooK)
LCCN: 2019910828

Printed in the United States of America

For further information contact Made for Success Publishing
+14255266480 or email service@madeforsuccess.net

FOR EVERY MAN!

Tom C

2 Tim 2:2

Tom G.

FOR EVERY MAN!

(ONE)

2 TIMES?

love.

Contents

Contents

Real-Life Discipleship

The Ordinary Man's Guide to Disciple-Making

TOM CHESHIRE & TOM GENSLER

Made for Grace
PUBLISHING

Risking Relationship

Today's culture frowns on men aspiring to be great because people fear what men will do with their influence. In fact, because of this fear, there is an intentional attack on masculine strength complete with negative labels, international marches and movements, cultural commentators, and energetic activists purposed to send a clear message: *masculinity is toxic.* While discouraging, you can't blame people for reacting this way. In fact, this reaction to men is justified on many levels because of the link between broken male culture and painful injustices affecting communities and countries around the world. Think about human trafficking, the orphan epidemic, domestic violence, epidemic levels of fatherlessness, and the symptomatic chaos and dysfunction all these create. And this is just the tip of the iceberg. Masculinity appears to be beaten up, on the brink of collapse, and in need of, not just resuscitation, but total transformation.

Enter Jesus.

Jesus' life and ministry became visible in the midst of a broken male culture—not dissimilar to the one we see on display today—that had misplaced greatness, manipulated religion to preserve masculine influence, and made others to suffer. More specifically, it marginalized women and children, making life difficult for them on every level. The prevailing mindset among the men surrounding Jesus was "Thank God I am not a woman, a child, or a Gentile." The cultural male of Jesus' time was not only encouraged in that thinking, but religious energy reinforced it. What did Jesus do about that? Read the Gospels, and you will see him deem it completely unacceptable, not of

> "Jesus turned and saw them following and said to them, 'What are you seeking?' And they said to him, "Rabbi" (which means Teacher), 'where are you staying?' He said to them, 'Come, and you will see.' So they came and saw where he was staying, and they stayed with him that day, for it was about the tenth hour."
> – John 1:38-39

God, and then completely flip it on its head, modeling and spawning a new movement of Spirit-empowered masculinity.

How exactly did he do that?

The short answer from the Gospels strongly suggests that Jesus embarked on a three-year season of relationship, intentionally spending time with twelve guys who would grow to reproduce a new masculine expression in Christ's image. During that time, they watched as Jesus protected, connected with, and, astonishingly, defended women. They listened in shock and awe as Jesus said, "Let the children come" and then watched him touch and bless them. Their jaws dropped and stomachs twisted as he told the story of the "Good" Samaritan. They watched him share the Good News of the Kingdom and spend time with the ethnically, morally, physically, and socially unacceptable. Religious men cringed. Women could not stop talking. Enemies consulted. The "least of these" rejoiced. The disciples, meanwhile, pondered what it all meant for them going forward.

The result of that modeling and purposeful investment in men would be twenty centuries of movement, impact, and legacy that all believers can trace their faith to down through the centuries. If that investment in those men does not happen, Christianity dies with Christ, or, at best, has a brief historic half-life like most other social phenomena. It would have passed away like so many reform movements common to that time. But Jesus' intentional invitation and impartation to men over a season of time assured him that they would not only carry on the work of the Kingdom but that they would, by all human measurement, far surpass his own relational footprint. Telling them as much, Jesus said: "Truly, truly, I say to you, whoever believes in me will also do the works that I do and greater works than these will he do because I am going to the Father." (John 14:12)

Did you catch that? *"Whoever believes… will do."*

Miraculously, Jesus reproduced his character and conduct in these men through a simple, intentional process, and then supported it with his own powerful example, a dispensation of ongoing leadership through His Spirit, a new community ecosystem (the church), and a commission to reproduce. His prophetic declaration of reproduction over his men was going to be an evolving fact in the days, weeks, and months to come. The first disciples could have never imagined in their wildest dreams the legacy their own lives would leave in response to Jesus' intentional mentoring and messaging. The Gospels reveal that there was frequency, helpful proximity, and transparency with Jesus as they walked, talked, connected, ate, slept, traveled, and ministered together over a three-year span. By contrast, Jesus knew this investment of time would lead to

Kingdom advance in the age preceding His return right down to you and me. The untrained rapscallions he recruited and trained would be present and accounted for themselves at ground zero in Jerusalem as chronicled in Acts 2: The moment that changed Western Civilization.

"But Peter, standing with the eleven, lifted up his voice and addressed them: "Men of Judea and all who dwell in Jerusalem, let this be known to you, and give ear to my words." (Acts 2:14)

Remember what Jesus said? *"Whoever believes ... will do."* And did they ever!

The real-life discipleship of men by Jesus is a powerful and profound story of transformation, legacy, and meaning as a man. Jesus shows us that the greatest impact a man can have—for good or for ill—is to reproduce himself in another man. But to do that Jesus' way, we must see clearly and simply what discipleship means in today's context in the lives of men. The book you hold in your hand is going to lay this out for you in simple, modern, relevant, and practical terms. Be grateful you chose this one!

Real-Life Discipleship is a stick of dynamite for any man who seeks to be a part of Jesus prophetic legacy and example of relational discipleship. The "Toms" on the front cover who laid out this powerful road map for you are not blowing out smoke or nice-sounding theology with zero functionality. You will find clarity, integrity, and effectiveness forged in the crucible of the relationships they formed with actual men they discipled and deployed. You can't give away what you don't possess. But more important than the wisdom only true experience provides, there is an economy of effort that you will love and appreciate. My good friends and your guides in this book have fought fights you never will and were kind enough to save you the pain in the pages that follow. Lastly, they know from doing ministry with men that victory for most men is one meaningful relationship away and that your legacy is the choice to pursue the relationships God has assigned uniquely to you. They don't shy away from this reality. They know the tension of spiritual battle is real, but so is the reward of not shrinking back. You are being called forward to risk relationship.

Someone's future is about to change.

Kenny Luck

Founder, Every Man Ministries
Author of *Dangerous Good: The Coming Revolution of Men Who Care* and *Sleeping Giant: No Move of God Without Men of God*
Executive Pastor of Leadership, Crossline Community Church

Who is RPM?

Relevant Practical Ministry for Men (RPM) was born in 2007 with the desire to serve the local church to mature their men in Christ to impact their families to change their communities for God's glory. Since then, we have organized and led over forty Iron Sharpens Iron (ISI) Men's Conferences impacting hundreds of local churches each year with over 30,000 men in attendance.

RPM's real passion is helping local churches take the next step of developing a custom men's ministry plan unique to their churches DNA. Our strategy is simple, we have led over thirty regional training events in the Midwest Illinois, Indiana, and Missouri called Ignite Pathway Men's Ministry Training impacting hundreds of local church pastors and leaders. Out of our training events we offer live coaching which has become the muscle and horsepower churches need to generate real momentum getting men *in, healthy, strong, and growing; and advancing the mission and vision of their local church and pastor.*

More personally, Tom Cheshire has discipled over 100 men with Tom Gensler being one of his direct disciples. Tom Gensler has gone on to invest in over 30 men himself.

Since 2013, the RPM team has organized and led a Father/Son Summer camp called Fathering Adventures. The camp has become an enormous success with hundreds of dads and sons being impacted. Fathers and sons spend the weekend being guided with just the right blend of biblical teaching, adventure, and one-on-one time that helps them deepen their bond and create memories that last a lifetime.

RPM has contributed chapters in two books *Engage: Building Your Church Based Ministry To Men* and *How To Disciple Men (Short & Sweet): 45 Proven Strategies From Experts On Ministry To Men.*

The RPM Team wakes every day with the burning desire to see the local church help their men grow spiritually, which will impact marriages, families, churches, and communities for God's glory.

CHAPTER 1

THE TOMS' TESTIMONY

THE YEAR WAS 1777, AND what was shaping up is what we now know as "The Battle of Saratoga." The British, who were the greatest army in the world at the time, were making plans to strategically control Upstate New York and isolate New England from the Southern colonies in an effort to decisively put an end to the Revolution.

The Continental Army was led by George Washington, who was inexperienced and underqualified. He was leading a group mostly made up of peasants and farmers who were amateurs at best. Some had never been formally trained; they were just ordinary men who believed in the idea of freedom.

At the start of the Revolutionary War, Washington had never led a large army into a major battle. During the war, the General chalked up more losses than wins. He struggled to overcome the discord and dissension amongst his men.

Right up until the Battle of Saratoga, Washington had carefully kept everything together—even when defeat was looking more certain with every passing day. He recognized that an alliance with the French was essential if the under-matched Continental Army was going to defeat the British in a head-to-head battle. Washington is said to have had the gifts of patience, perseverance and self-awareness (to name a few), and he knew what battles had to be won.

Historians say he had a knack for taking people in, who seemed like they couldn't achieve great things. These types of people were often written off by everyone around them, but under Washington's leadership, they rose to the challenge. He was a leader who found the right balance at just the right time. He displayed confidence in his fellow citizen-soldiers.

Washington was unqualified, over-matched and fearful, yet he led an army of ordinary men with great courage.

George Washington's challenges during the Revolutionary War make for a great parallel for men in the church today who feel an internal pull from the Holy Spirit to do more than they feel qualified to do. Men like you, who want to be involved in investing in other men spiritually but feel inexperienced, inadequate and undertrained. You may have found yourself saying, "I have never done anything like this!" Let us assure you; you are not alone in these feelings.

Just like the ragtag group of men that Washington led to a decisive victory over the British with no qualification apart from a belief in something bigger than themselves, you have what it takes. All that is necessary is that you believe in the idea of advancing the Kingdom of God, and recognize that all it takes is godly men working in conjunction with the Holy Spirit to reproduce more godly men.

Discipleship is not easy. Failure is ripe, and rejection is high. It's going to take patience, perseverance, self-awareness and whole lot of holy boldness to invest in men the way Jesus did. Without discipleship, it is near impossible to keep growing in maturity. Chances are, either you have experienced the difficulty of walking this life without a mentor, or you know someone who has. If we want to see godly men rise up in the church, we have to start by stepping out where we feel inadequate. Be the man you wished you had when you started walking with the Lord or the brother you see your friends struggling to find. When we begin to disciple other men and walk with them intentionally, we will see a ragtag army rise up, just like George Washington's.

Tom Cheshire's Testimony

It was December 1997, and my wife's friend's husband approached me after church. He awkwardly asked if I would like to go with him to a conference called Promise Keepers in August, and I awkwardly accepted his invitation.

The truth is, I was hiding some pretty significant sin: I had been flirty with my secretary, I was watching porn in the darkness of my basement with increased regularity, and was going to topless bars anytime I traveled. This friend had no idea of my secret life, nor did anyone I work with. My wife, Jan, knew "something" was not right, but my lies had been effective thus far.

I remember thinking to myself; *I will use this conference to help myself finally break free from my lustful struggles.* I reasoned it would give me time to stop all the crap and get my stuff together. The Holy Spirit was clearly working in my heart; He brought conviction, making me conscious of the fact that everything I was doing and involved in was grieving God.

* * *

In January of 1998, my company hosted a management retreat to work on leadership and team building. A fellow manager approached me out of the blue, shared that he knew I was a Christian and shared that he was as well. We agreed to start meeting to do a bible study in his office once a week.

Why did he approach me, and why did we end up having a conversation about God? Well, I had a reputation at work, but not the kind of reputation you may be thinking. I was known around the office as "the Christian." So, this guy sought me out to do life together.

Considering my distance from God at the time, my first thought was not that Holy Spirit was doing the connecting; my first thought was, *How weird is it that a somewhat random man invites me to a Promise Keepers conference then this guy at work asks me to study the Bible?* I honestly did not connect it to God when it was happening. Though you can likely see God's hand in this clearly as you read, sin had completely blinded me to it back then. In fact, I made excuse after excuse about why I couldn't join him for a bible study. However, he was very patient with me, and while he continued to ask, I continued to avoid him.

Stopping this runaway train was now appearing to be much harder than I thought it would be. While I did make some effort to stop some of my destructive behaviors, for some reason, I continued to flirt and exchange emails with my secretary. Sometimes I initiated them, sometimes she did. I guess I found it all rather "exciting." Here was yet another sign that when the reward of our goal (lust) blinds us to the risk of our sin (consequences), we are in deep.

We continued on with our inappropriate communications online, as well as interactions in person. It seemed to be a mutual feeling that perhaps we might actually someday have a legitimate sexual encounter.

Fast forward to July: while I had slowed way down on the porn and topless bars, the communications with my secretary had increased in intensity, and the actual physical act seemed to be looming closer and closer with each email and conversation. I left for a business trip to Houston, Texas, and would be away from the office for a week. One night, I received a rather urgent phone call from a friend in my department. He went on to explain that it appeared my secretary had gone to HR and filed a complaint against me concerning my behavior towards her. He said he didn't know what was going to happen, but it appeared I was in big trouble.

I decided to take the next flight back home and was told I needed to head immediately to the HR manager as soon as I got in to have an emergency meeting. Our meeting was short and to the point, and I was told this was a severe accusation and sent home for a two-week suspension while the investigation took place.

I remember getting into my car and driving home, racked with fear. How was I going to explain this to my wife? I pulled over on the side of the road in a panic and sat in my car, crying like a baby. Everything started flashing in front of my eyes, and I finally realized what terrible choices I had made. I had walked away from God. I sat there for a long time, desperately trying to come up with some sort of way out from this mess. Even though I had said I was going to fix this—which seems like a noble thing to do from the outside—it had gone horribly wrong in the fact that I had relied solely on me, myself and I. I had told God I would clean myself up and come back to Him once I was worthy. Again, what is obvious to me now (and you as you read) is the huge error in that sort of thinking, but in the midst of sin, I was blinded to the misplaced logic.

I've historically never been one who was big on the whole "hearing from God" thing, but right in the middle of that "dark night of the soul" moment, I had an overwhelming sense of His presence. I somehow finally understood that He was the only one who could rescue me. It was as if Jesus were asking, "What do you want me to do for you?" He made it clear that I was at a pivotal fork in the road in my life. I remember getting out of my car, falling on my knees and crying out to God to save me from my sin. I had always been skeptical of other people's stories that shared how they felt a weight being lifted off them, but that was precisely what I felt. I understood that there would be consequences for my sin—that He wasn't just going to make all this go away—but there was such a deep-seated peace that I knew His grace was sufficient. God impressed two things on me that day: trust Him, and tell the truth, no matter how hard either of those would be in the coming hours, weeks and years.

What unfolded over the next couple days were some of the hardest and darkest places I have ever been in my life. Coming completely clean with my wife shattered her heart in ways no one should ever have to experience. By God's grace, she stayed with me through it all. As hard as it was, I really believe she could see that God was transforming her husband's heart right in front of her eyes. While she was skeptical and suspicious for a long time, she couldn't deny the hand of God working in my life. I vowed to tell the whole truth and nothing but the truth throughout the investigation. So much so, that at one point, the HR manager said to me, "In all the years I have been working in this position, I have never seen anyone be as completely honest or own up to something like you have." I knew it was God and God alone that was giving me the strength and ability to walk through this.

At this point you may be thinking to yourself, *Okay, this is good and all but what in blue blazes does this have to do with a book on discipleship?!*

Remember the friend who invited me to the Promise Keepers conference back in December? Coincidentally, the end of my two-week suspension ended as I boarded a bus headed to the conference, and this friend was the first person I shared with about everything that happened—the good, bad and the ugly. The significance of that trip and that man inviting me would turn out to be more than I could ever imagine or hope. On the way up there, a complete stranger sat down next to me. His smile and sweet demeanor were alarmingly unpretentious, and he begged to hear what was going on in my life. I am sure he had no idea what God was about to do through him as he sat down next to me and asked the simple question, "How are you doing, friend?"

His name was Scott Brindley, and the friendship that was born on that bus has become the sweetest friendship I have ever known to this day. I don't think he would have called this process discipleship, even though that is exactly what it was. Scott simply saw a man in need of another godly man to walk alongside him and help heal his marriage... not to mention his *life*. That is what godly men do when they see that God has clearly opened a door, and he was obedient to that call.

Scott spent the first few months of our relationship seeing me in person every single day. He opened God's word, listened to me and applied Scripture and understanding like no one I have ever met. Scott was the walking epitome of grace lived out. He took on the role of a spiritual father to me and walked it out until the day he passed on August 8th, 2013.

Remember the friend from work who had asked me to participate in a bible study with him in his office? His name is Jim Talley, and he showed up at my house every morning for two weeks straight during my suspension. He introduced me to spiritual disciplines and a love I still have to this day for daily devotionals. Jim also discipled me with intentionality and invested in me both on the job and at home. He, like Scott, was instrumental in showing me how to apply God's word in the workplace, as well at home in my roles of husband and father. Unfortunately, he got transferred to another job, but we still stay in touch. I continually recount to him how he loved me at my lowest and reminded me daily of who I was in Christ.

Over the last 20 years, there have been many other men who have invested in me, and once I got to a healthier place, they encouraged me to do the same.

It was out of this brokenness that God helped me see I wasn't a lone wolf in His church. My eyes were opened to the sad reality that His church is filled with men who behave like I used to, acting the part of a godly man while hiding sin that was looking to blow them up. It is through being open and transparent about my struggle with the sin of sexual immorality that I started a journey to invest in other men, and God saw fit to use me to start a ministry that would empower local churches to see men properly mature in Christ.

My story is never very far from my heart as I move from day to day, and I am constantly reminded of who I was and what God did in my heart. My miraculous transformation is the motivation when times are hard, money is tight and I'm believing the lie that I should just do something else. If God's grace is sufficient for me, then it is certainly sufficient for you.

Tom Gensler's Testimony

In 2007, I found myself living the American Dream. I had the perfect job, a beautiful wife, a wonderful home and everything I needed to live a comfortable life. On the outside, I was the person that others looked up to and appeared to have it all together. On the inside, I was fearful, hated my life and was completely confused about what it meant to be a real man—a godly man. The straw that finally broke the camel's back was discovering my wife was involved in an emotional affair.

Our dream life came tumbling down overnight, and I was left to face some pretty harsh realities. We agreed to separate with the understanding that neither of us wanted a divorce. Initially, I found it hard to believe that after working so hard to provide my wife with everything she wanted, she would go and cheat on me. While sitting in our home one evening during our separation, I cried out to God seeking answers as I looked back over the past four years, wondering where I went wrong. As you'll read further on in my story, the Holy Spirit gave me clarity that would ultimately change my life forever.

* * *

Lisa and I were married in 2004, right after I completed my bachelor's degree in business management. I had just begun pursuing a Master of Divinity degree to work in full-time ministry. After only a year of seminary, the pressure to start a family and make "real" money took its toll, and I left graduate school to step back into the family business: running a successful multi-line car dealership in the Midwest.

Just a year later, it felt as if I had "made it." I was managing the back end of a car dealership, handling millions of dollars and reaping the benefit of massive success. I had the job everyone else wanted, with all the benefits to go along with it: the big office with a glass door, a brand-new company car, free gas, an expense account and loads of flexibility that ensured I was able to be where I wanted to be when I wanted to be there. I had arrived!

I tell folks now that the song from the movie *Fireproof,* "It's a Slow Fade" perfectly described my life and marriage during this time. From 2005 to 2007, we slowly faded away from God. We were not making church attendance a priority, our prayer life ceased and we stopped spending time together talking about life and God. We pulled away from our support network of fellow believers and began hanging around old friends who coerced us back into the world that forces you to consume and focus on yourself. We started drinking alcohol again, cussing like sailors and buying stuff like our happiness was going to be found in the next big purchase. I remember purchasing my dream car during this time without Lisa's approval, a Cherry Red Mitsubishi 3000GT VR-4 Twin Turbo.

Right before I discovered my wife's affair, I had become a jerk who thought only of himself and how much money he could make. The power trip I was on at work followed me home. No one challenged me on the job; it was my way or the highway. I had the ability to make or break your career. If I liked you, I could assure you job security, good pay and flexible work hours. If I didn't like you, well… let's just say you weren't very excited to come into the office. Looking back on this time of our lives, it is clear we did not have a marriage—it was merely an arrangement that ensured I could have all my needs met.

As you can imagine, when I discovered that my wife was having an affair, it completely knocked me off my high horse and I fell flat on the ground.

I found myself sitting alone in our newly remodeled house that could have been on an HGTV show, wondering how I had gotten to this point. We had worked so hard to make this house a home, and it was just the way we wanted it to be; the only problem now was that she wasn't there to enjoy it with me. Feeling depressed and defeated, I began to reflect on how we had fallen so hard. I distinctly recall crying out to God and hearing him say, "Tom, it's you… *you're* the problem." It was clear as day, and it continued. "Let me work on you first. Sure, Lisa has done some things wrong, but the problem is you, Tom. Until you let me clean you up, nothing is going to change." This revelation from God shook me to my core and caused me to stop pointing the finger and begin accepting responsibility for all the brokenness in our marriage and my life.

I went to our local church at the time, who knew Lisa and I were separated, and sat down to talk with our pastor. I cut straight to the chase and said, "I know what is wrong with me."

"What is it?" he replied, a puzzled look spreading across his face.

"I do not know how to be a godly man! For starters, I do not know how to lead my wife spiritually. I certainly do not know how to be a man with integrity in the workplace. I have no idea what it means to do things God's way."

"Are you sure you are saved?"

"I am sure I am saved. I understand salvation and what Jesus has done for mankind and my sins. What I do know I need is discipleship; I need another man to show me what it looks like to live out biblical manhood."

I don't know very many people who walk straight into a church and ask for someone to disciple them, but that was all I knew to do. They directed me to attend my first *Iron Sharpens Iron* men's conference in the spring of 2008, where I discovered the man leading the conference made himself available to meet with other men. Tom Cheshire and I began a discipling relationship soon after, and for the next year and a half, I drove 45 minutes every week to sit with him and learn how to be a godly man.

By the grace of God and excellent Christian counseling, Lisa and I worked through and repaired our broken marriage. We began to share struggles openly with each other and dedicated ourselves to learning more about the other's needs. One of the biggest helps was reading *The Five Love Languages* by Gary Chapman. We learned how to give and receive love in ways that were in line with the way we were wired. It was revolutionary to me to learn my wife did not receive love the way I wanted to show it, which was by working hard and doing things for her. She wanted me to shower her with positive words of affirmation, which happens to be something that is not easy for me to do. But I have now learned that because it's what she needs from me, I have to get over myself and serve and love her.

God used another man taking his time to invest in me spiritually to transform my marriage, my workplace and our entire lives. I went from a controlling, angry jerk of a boss to a kind and life-giving presence that others liked being around. Discipleship taught me what it meant to be a godly man—a man that accepted responsibility for my marriage, my career and my problem. A man who rejects the internal pull to be passive when life gets hard. A man of action who leads courageously through the difficulties we all face. A man who lives with an eternal mindset that understands that while I may not see the benefit to all I am doing now, I am ultimately storing up treasures in heaven.

God went on to do miraculous things through my life and story. I eventually started up a prayer group at work, and used the office to disciple other men and teach them what I learned from Tom Cheshire. A co-worker was even saved through hearing what God had done in my life! Our marriage has blossomed into a beautiful work of art—we now have five children (Ruby, Moses, Gabriel, Shiloh and Selah) and are serving full-time in the very ministry that God used to begin the transformation in my life all those years ago.

God brought me to the end of myself by allowing my career and marriage to bottom out. Then, through listening to his still small voice, he called out to me. And when He did, thankfully I was looking for Him. He has guided me to the right men at the right times to disciple me into Christ-likeness. Tom Cheshire taught me godly manhood. Travis Bodden has been a trusted friend and confidant I can share anything with. Jeff Schulte taught me how to look under the hood of my life to understand why I am the way I am. Bob Bolin is a mature, older gentleman that is quite possibly the nicest man I have ever had the privilege of knowing. Not to mention the countless other men who may have had a timely conversation with me or spent time helping me through a difficult situation.

God has used discipleship through the context of one-on-one relationships with other men to change the course of my life. I know He will in your life as well, if you are open and listening for His direction.

CHAPTER 2

Defining Discipleship

I F YOU WERE IN A ROOM full of Christians right now, and you asked them how they came to know Jesus and/or grew in maturity, we would venture a bet that almost everyone would answer that it involved another person investing in them. Testimonies like ours are far more common than you might think. With that in mind, this chapter is going to give you some tools for moving forward: definitions, statistics, the most common barriers or obstacles, and some practical applications for biblical discipleship (which is disciple-making).

If discipleship is the process of making disciples, then what exactly is a disciple?

A disciple is simply a follower or student of a teacher or leader.

Now that we've defined discipleship, let's talk about what we see in the passage above, commonly known as the Great Commission. This is the mandate from Jesus to His disciples to spread the gospel to the ends of the earth. This is not only written to his original audience, the twelve disciples, but it is also written to every single person who has been rescued and redeemed by the grace of Jesus Christ. If this is the biggest mandate on followers of Christ, why are we not bearing the fruit of this command?

> "And Jesus came and said to them, 'All authority in heaven and on earth has been given to me. Go therefore and **make disciples** of all nations, baptizing them in the name of the Father and of the Son and of the Holy Spirit, teaching them to observe all that I have commanded you. And behold, I am with you always, to the end of the age.
> – Matthew 28:18-20 (emphasis added)"

We've found one of the key components to helping churches begin to develop a discipleship culture in their body is that they must first work through the answer to the following question: *what is discipleship, exactly?*

There are a lot of factors that contribute to this confusion, a big one being that the very word itself is somewhat of a "Christianese" buzzword in today's churches. We would argue that discipleship has become the "catch-all" drawer of everything we do in church. You might remember the word *missional* doing the same thing a few years back—a word we loved to throw around in conversation, but never actually understood what the word meant. But we digress; we aren't here to tackle that term, we have enough on our plate with discipleship!

First, let's talk about what discipleship *isn't*.

Pastor, we hate to tell you this, but your preaching—as good as it is—is *not* in itself, discipleship. Though disciple means learner or student, and you are teaching, your Sunday sermons don't take the place of meeting people in person and teaching them about what it looks like to live a godly life. Please don't get us wrong; we are not saying preaching and exhorting the Word of God is not critical to a follower of Jesus Christ, because it is. Your preaching, pastor, is where you instill the value of God's word to your people. It is where you lay out biblical truth for them. But it is not discipleship. We do want to encourage you that preaching is simply a part of a bigger plan to intentionally move followers into a deeper, more personal relationship with Jesus and others, which is creating a discipleship culture.

We often fill our schedules with "church" activities that are not discipleship, i.e., Sunday school, mid-week gatherings, prayer meetings, and book studies. As we mentioned with preaching, please understand we are not saying that these aren't good things. In fact, if they are done with strategy and intentionality, they can be a vital part of your discipleship "culture." However, these activities and classes will never replace the act of meeting with someone one-on-one in order to grow and mature.

Now, hear us out here: we don't profess to be biblical scholars, or even highly-schooled professionals. Honestly, we mostly relate to the description you see in Acts 4:13, "Now when they saw the boldness of Peter and John, and perceived that they were uneducated, common men, they were astonished. And they recognized they had been with Jesus."

By reading our stories in the previous chapter, we hope you understand why we believe in the value of discipleship. How the Bible defines discipleship is of utmost importance to us, and frankly, it should be important to you as well.

We believe biblical discipleship is doing life together—it's being relational with at least one other man for a period of time. We believe you can see it being lived out in both the Old and New Testament. A great example is how the Apostle Paul took young Timothy under his wing. The introduction in 1st and 2nd Timothy says it all: "To Timothy, my true child in the faith" and "To Timothy, my beloved child."

These introductions speak to a very close relationship. Paul and Timothy were not related, but because of Paul spending time with and making strategic investments into Timothy, they had a deep love for each other. Discipleship is messy, honest, open and transparent time spent with others. It involves confessing sin, forgiveness and fighting together with accountability. Most importantly, it is built on the foundation of reading and applying the truth of God's word in our lives.

The fruit of discipleship is simple: becoming more and more like Christ as we are maturing in our faith. The other aspect of discipleship is that we must be faithful, available and teachable. These characteristics will mark us for life if we truly are walking in relationship with other men because they speak to commitment, discipline and humility—of which we must be lifelong learners.

There are many people, books and studies that have, and are continually influencing us. We will give credit and point to those as we use information from them throughout this book.

The State of Discipleship, which is a Barna Report produced in partnership with The Navigators, is one of the books we will reference in this chapter pretty heavily. Barna Group has released countless studies and gathered overwhelming statistics in such a way that they bring about unbiased, timely information for the masses. This study is no different, as their sample size is both impressive and extensive. The Navigators are the steadfast ministry of discipleship. Many men we have come to know and deeply respect find their roots in The Navigators, and I (Tom Cheshire) have personally benefitted from their Bible studies as well. In fact, I have taken my family through the entire Bible using Navigator resources.

In the opening executive summary of *The State of Discipleship*, the very first paragraph says, "A critical component of this study is to define 'discipleship.' The concept is familiar to many, but a widely accepted definition remains elusive. Although it may seem a mere technicality, accurate and relative terminology and a clear definition are important first steps toward ensuring a church or ministry can effectively grow disciples."

Amen, Barna!

You see, even Barna Group and The Navigators know that you can't make disciples unless you agree on the definition of what discipleship or disciple-making is. While we think there is a lot of useful data in this book, it still falls short for us. Why? Well, it gives us a definition that answers the "what" question, but not the "how" question. In fact, this is a big reason we have felt compelled to write this very book. There is a ton of good material that defines the "what" perspective of discipleship, but neglects or completely misses the "how." We feel a lot of the material out there today—and believe us, there is plenty out there—falls more on the theory side rather than application. We are living and active lab rats on the practical side of discipleship. You see other men have invested in our spiritual growth, and we both still have men investing in us for the purpose of allowing us to see how the gospel is working itself out in their lives. That compels us to turn and do the same to other men God is bringing in our lives. It is 2 Timothy 2:2 in action "…and what you have heard from me in the presence of many witnesses entrust to faithful men, who will be able to teach others also."

Here is how Barna broke down the data on "defining" discipleship. We have included the actual graphs in the book as well as Barna Group's description or definition (page 28) of who made up those groups. They have three distinct groups in the first segment; all church leaders, mainline leaders and non-mainline leaders (page 28). The other segment also has three distinct groups, all Christian adults, non-practicing Christians and practicing Christians (page 29). For more details about who and how those groupings are formed and counted, we encourage you to purchase this book and read on for yourself.

1. Preferred Terms for Discipleship
(% among church leaders)

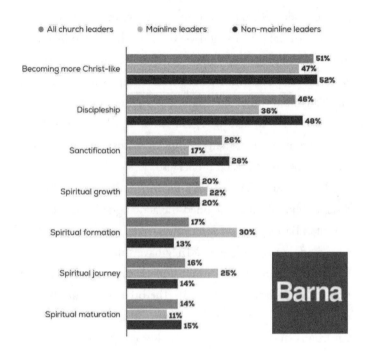

2. Preferred Terms for Discipleship
(% among Christian adults)

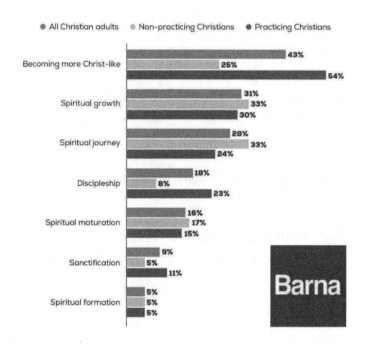

● All Christian adults   ○ Non-practicing Christians   ● Practicing Christians

Becoming more Christ-like
- 43%
- 25%
- 54%

Spiritual growth
- 31%
- 33%
- 30%

Spiritual journey
- 28%
- 33%
- 24%

Discipleship
- 18%
- 8%
- 23%

Spiritual maturation
- 16%
- 17%
- 15%

Sanctification
- 9%
- 5%
- 11%

Spiritual formation
- 5%
- 5%
- 5%

Barna

DEFINITIONS

Denominational Segments

Mainline: includes American Baptist Churches, Episcopal, Evangelical Lutheran Church of America, United Church of Christ, United Methodist Church and Presbyterian Church, USA

Non-Mainline: includes Protestant churches not included in mainline denominations

Other Christians: self-identified Christians who do not identify as attending a Mainline or Non-mainline church as described above

Leader Segments

Senior Pastors: church leaders who are the senior leader of their congregation

Discipleship Leaders: church leaders whose ministry specifically focuses on discipleship

All Church Leaders: senior pastors and discipleship leaders combined

Faith Segments

Self-Identified Christians: those who select "Christian" when asked to identify their religion; also sometimes called "all Christians"

Practicing Christians: self-identified Christians who have attended a church service, other than for a special occasion such as a wedding or holiday, at least once during the past month and who say their faith is very important in their life today

Non-Practicing Christians: self-identified Christians who do not qualify as "practicing" under the criteria above

Navigator Alumni: respondents who have participated in a Navigators discipleship program

Again, quoting *The State of Discipleship*, in the opening chapter it reads, "Before we can understand the state of discipleship, we must ask, 'What is discipleship?' The clearest insight from this study… is that the definition of discipleship is unclear!"

Though this still left us with no concrete answers, what that affirms in us is the answer to why what we are trying to do is so dang hard!

The majority of the data from Barna reveals that amongst Christians and church leaders, there is no consistency in how we define discipleship and what it practically looks like lived out. We need to come to a concrete definition of discipleship that everyone can agree on, and then we need clear parameters on what producing mature believers looks like.

Quoting Barna again, here is what you can see from the graphs above.

"The most common term selected by Christian adults and church leaders alike to describe the process of spiritual growth is 'becoming more Christ-like.'"

You see that the most common term or definition for discipleship is the "process of spiritual growth." This is precisely why we would say that discipleship has become the catch-all drawer, and we throw everything we do into it. When we meet with pastors and leaders, we eliminate that very response as one of the choices for defining discipleship. We do this not because spiritual growth and becoming more Christ-like aren't good and right goals, but rather because they are vague. We would say that the definition of discipleship *is* the process of spiritual growth, *not* a characteristic of what you should look like. We would put the Barna answer as the fruit or by-product of discipleship.

If you look at Jesus' life and interaction in the New Testament, he isn't teaching them by simply saying, "Be more like me." He is living his life according to the will of the Father and telling the disciples to do what they see him doing. Even Jesus claims he is not doing anything of his own accord; rather, he is doing what he sees the Father doing.

We see both the relational and the "lived out" aspect between Jesus and

> " So Jesus said to them, 'Truly, truly, I say to you, the Son can do nothing of his own accord, but only what he sees the Father doing. For whatever the Father does, that the Son does likewise. "
> – John 5:19

the Father that applies to Jesus and his disciples, so why do we think differently today? Kennon Vaughan, the founder of Downline Ministries in Memphis, TN says, "Jesus spent 85% of His time during His three-year public ministry with 12 men." This, of course, would include time they are with the masses together, but 85% of the time they are with Jesus.

We don't want to write your definition of discipleship for you, but we *do* want to point to the entirety of Scripture. We do have our own definition, which is based on our examination of the Scriptures combined with how it has practically played out in our lives. We would say discipleship is **one man investing in one or more men by walking alongside them on a regular basis, allowing them to see how we pray, open the Bible and practically apply those truths in our lives, marriages, families, workplaces, communities and churches.** We call this "real-life" discipleship; the kind that we see Jesus and countless other men in the Bible giving us an example of in their lives.

What we also see from the word is that discipleship is about doing; it's about action. It's about a life being lived out that defines becoming more Christ-Like. Moses didn't take Joshua up on the mountain with him and say, "You need to be more like me." He simply takes him along and allows Joshua to see how he communes with God and how he leads. When it is time for Joshua to lead the Israelites to the Promised Land, he does it by remembering and mimicking what he witnessed Moses, his discipler, doing. Moses modeled the point we are emphasizing to you. Doing life together and bringing Joshua along is an example of how many things are more caught than taught. There is no short cut to allowing others to be with us and see how we live and react to everyday life.

It is no surprise as to what Barna came up with as the two main obstacles or barriers to discipleship—at least it was no surprise to us.

What were they? Busyness and commitment.

Gasp. Say it ain't so, Pappy.

> "All the groups Barna interviewed – Christian adults, church leaders, exemplars and educators – agree on the two most significant barriers to spiritual growth: the general 'busyness' of life and a lack of commitment to discipleship."

Yikes.

Real-life discipleship, as we previously defined above, is a sacrifice in today's world. It takes a commitment from both the leader/teacher as well as the follower/student. They both only have 24 hours in a day. For Jim Talley to show up at my (Tom Cheshire's) house every morning at six-o-clock for weeks took sacrifice, and for Scott Brindley to meet with me every week for years took a huge commitment.

The Barna study again pointed out what we see as obvious issues with the way our churches and leaders view and define discipleship. Barna said there was a strong disagreement between church leaders and Christian adults on the magnitude of these barriers. What the study essentially revealed was that busyness was the more prevalent issue with church leaders (85%), while adult Christians rated it 23%. Here is another quote from the book that tells the real story and simultaneously breaks my heart.

> "In addition to low rates of participation in discipleship activities, further evidence of general spiritual apathy comes from the one in ten Christians who say their spiritual growth is 'not too' or 'not at all' important. Two-thirds of these say they are comfortable with where they are spiritually. Among a significant number of Christians today, there is simply no drive to prioritize spiritual growth."

We understand that the statement above may not shock you, probably because you most likely fall into the one out of ten or two-thirds group. Hopefully, by the end of this book, the Holy Spirit will have kicked you in the seat of the pants, and you'll move into the nine out of ten and one-third group. If you are a pastor or leader reading this, we hope that it breaks your heart as well (in the best possible way). We hope that heartbreak then drives you to ask, "How do we change this statistic?"

To quote the great theologian, Dr. Phil, "How's what you're doing now working for you?"

You see, it is data like this that pours gas on our already white-hot fire to be a resource to you: the local church. If the current structure most churches are using to mature people spiritually was working, then we wouldn't be seeing the spiritual apathy and passivity in Christians that we see. We wouldn't have a fatherlessness epidemic affecting millions of children. Drug use likely wouldn't be at an all-time high. If the current plan to offer preaching on Sunday and a Sunday school class were maturing our church members, then we would see hearts being changed impacting families and communities around this country and world. Pastor's EVERY opportunity to both teach and learn are good; however, not EVERY opportunity to teach or learn is real-life discipleship.

We want to end this chapter with some positive ways you can bring forth change in your local church. The same things apply if you are a pastor, a lay-leader, or simply a follower of Jesus who wants to grow. We might be stating the obvious in the following paragraphs, but sometimes that is exactly what we need to make changes. Change is going to require the same things, regardless of which group you find yourself in right now. It is going to require sacrifice, time, consistency and commitment, which are the foundation for any discipline. You don't become a marathon runner by running once a month for five minutes. 1 Timothy 4:7-8 says this, "Have nothing to do with irreverent, silly myths. Rather train yourself for godliness; for while bodily training is of some value, godliness is of value in every way, as it holds promise for the present life and also for the life to come."

Barna hits on two main points about a healthy culture of discipleship, but again falls a little short on the "how." Barna says, "A healthy culture of discipleship, according to exemplar leaders, appears to be created by 1) senior leadership and 2) a clear plan."

We couldn't agree more. However, in order to understand "how," you must be in an active discipleship relationship with other men with the goal of releasing those men to go on and disciple other men. You must have a plan for what this looks like for you and those in your church to train and grow in godliness.

Pastors, if you don't live this out in your church, then we can say, with a high level of certainty, that your people will not live it out either. You may be saying to yourself, "You don't know how much I have on my plate! I just don't have the margin to meet with a few men on a regular basis." That obviously has some level of truth to it; no one who knows the life of pastor ever thinks, "Gee I wonder what they do with all the free time between Sundays and their one day of work?" However, in some ways, we need to read between the lines of what Barna states statistically. The reality that so many fail to see the need to prioritize spiritual growth is because it is not being modeled by our leadership. Ask any parent, "Which do you think most influences and produces results in your children: what you tell them to do, or what they observe you doing?" We are sure the resounding answer would be the latter.

> "...and what you have heard from me in the presence of many witnesses entrust to faithful men, who will be able to teach others also.
> – 2 Timothy 2:2

It is surely not by accident that Jesus lived day in and day out with his disciples, causing them to observe all He commanded, but this example has been lost in most western churches.

Men, of all walks of life and calling: you can do this! We not only want to give you the challenge to step up and the encouragement to do so, we want to give you what we think are some basic, practical ways to help you make the adjustment from disciple to being a disciple-maker, carry out the great commission, and go on to help others do the same.

CHAPTER 3

Do You Have What It Takes?

Back in February of 1998, I (Tom Gensler) went to Basic Training for the United States Army at Fort Benning in Georgia. It was nearly a year before this date that I signed on the dotted line and began preparing. I knew it would be the hardest challenge I had ever accepted up to this point in my young 17 years of life. In fact, I had several family members wonder if I had what it would take to complete the grueling three-month training to receive the title of United States Army Infantryman.

I remember my Army recruiter giving specific details on how prepared I needed to be. He had said I needed to be able to run two miles in a specified time, as well as a certain amount of sit-ups and push-ups in two minutes. So, I went out for a run every day and many nights to prepare for this challenge. I adjusted my diet to help me run better and do more push-ups and sit-ups. The recruiter also told me, "You'll be getting up at 4:30 am every day, so you better prepare yourself." For three months, I began getting up earlier and earlier. At first, getting up that early seemed impossible, but the more I did it, the more my body adjusted.

As the day drew closer for me to ship off to basic training, I knew all this preparation would pay off... or so I thought. I arrived at Fort Benning, Georgia in February of 1998, and immediately realized the training and commitment I signed up for was much more difficult than I was first led to believe.

To my surprise, we spent the first few weeks not in basic training, but in what's called "reception." Reception basically means you're in a holding pattern, waiting for your training to start. I remember asking if the days we spent in reception counted towards our basic training, and the answer was a resounding "No."

I made it through the several weeks of reception only to discover the first morning of basic training began with garbage can lids being banged against each other at 4:30 in the morning. I thought to myself; *The recruiter was right about the time we would wake up, but not how they woke us up*. We laced up our shoes and went out for morning Physical Training (PT), which consisted of doing exercise for longer and harder than you have ever thought possible. We wrapped up our first morning of PT with a five-mile run. Excuse me?! I was told we started out at two miles! I literally sucked wind for those additional three miles, but I made it. My first morning of basic training was in the books; now I just had to survive three more months!

Eighty-nine days later, I made it. I graduated with course number 024-98 to earn the title of United States Army Infantryman.

Discipling another man is a lot like my basic training experience. You can prepare for many different scenarios and experiences, but until you put yourself out there and begin a relationship, you won't really know what to expect. Sure, there will be many life experiences you have lived and can re-teach a younger man in the faith. What you have experienced will be very valuable as you re-invest. However, there will also be many things that come up that you did not think of, or may not have directly experienced. That's okay—Jesus Christ is our master teacher, and I share the same truth with the men that call me looking for wisdom—He has already dealt with everything we are dealing with. Sure, it may not be the same exact situation, but the root issues such as anger, lying,

41

temptation, greed and failure are things Jesus dealt with, and His response should be our response. Life has a way of presenting obstacles, but we must take them on in love, advance the cause of Christ, and make the name of Jesus famous, regardless of what the enemy presents.

* * *

This chapter is titled, "Do you have what it takes?" We are going to do our best to help you figure out where you are at in your walk and if you should first be discipled or are ready to be a disciple-maker. When I (Tom Gensler) first started taking steps closer to Christ and learning about biblical manhood, my life was significantly shaped by the teaching of Dr. Robert Lewis. He is the creator of Men's Fraternity, which is a series of DVD studies designed to help men embrace a bolder and more noble concept of manhood.

In one of Dr. Lewis's teaching sessions, he shares a story where he recalls the first time he met the famed football coach Jackie Sherrill. At the time, Sherrill was the linebacker coach at the University of Arkansas, where Lewis played football. Jackie had just had his team soundly beaten, and he was mad—real mad. Everyone on the team knew he did pretty weird stuff to motivate his team, and this situation was no different. After the game ended and the players were back in the locker room, Sherrill called a team huddle.

"Guys, we're not going to make it this season unless you look deep down within yourself and get tougher. I mean, a lot tougher. You know how tough you need to get?"

He walked over to a locker and pulled out a little pail that looked like he had just stolen it from a kid at the beach. He brought it over into the middle of the room, reached down, and pulled up a baby alligator. There was an audible gasp as the men racked their brains to figure out what he could possibly be doing.

"Let me show how tough you're going to have to get."

He unzipped his pants, dropped his drawers, turned around and let that alligator take a big chunk into his rear end. Another audible gasp filled the room. With the alligator hanging off his rear end, he continued to walk around, looking at each of his players.

"*This* is how tough you've got to get. This tough! You think you can be this tough?!" he yelled.

After a few moments, he turned around and poked the alligator in the eyes. It immediately released, relaxing into Jackie's hands.

"Okay boys, who wants to be next?"

A big lineman in the back raised his hand and said, "Uh, I will, coach, if you don't poke me in the eyes to make me let go."

* * *

Now that we have lightened the mood and made you crack a smile, let's shift our focus to the real spiritual battle taking place for the souls of men.

Ephesians 6:11 reminds us, "Finally, be strong in the Lord and in the strength of his might. Put on the whole armor of God, that you may be able to stand against the schemes of the devil." As good, God-fearing men like yourself advance to make the name of Jesus known in our cities and communities, we must remember the following truth the Apostle Peter shares in 1 Peter 5:8, "Your adversary the devil prowls around like a roaring lion, seeking someone to devour." Not only does he seek to devour you, but he is seeking to devour the legacy you are passing down amongst the next generations. John 10:10 says, "The thief comes only to steal and kill and destroy; I came that they may have life, and have it abundantly."

Men, your legacy to the next generations needs to be your example of what a godly man looks like. We are tasked with raising the next generation of God's people. So, to say we have a lot on the line is an understatement! A legacy of loving God, loving our wives, and raising children that have a vibrant relationship with Jesus when they leave our watch is vital. Satan wants to destroy your legacy; he wants to wipe it (and you) from the face of the earth.

We believe the hinge point in our culture for whether we draw closer or further from God is its men. We also believe Satan understands this. He knows that if a man gets his heart right with God and he catches the vision that Jesus models for manhood, then his marriage, his children, his workplace and community will follow. However, Satan knows if a man drifts from God and falls for his schemes, then his marriage will most likely drift that way, his children might grow up not knowing God, and he is not the example for manhood at work or in his community.

Satan has lots of sneaky plans to destroy—one of which is the corporate ladder. He wants to draw men away with what we call *the 3 B's*: the billfold, the ballfield, and the bedroom. A busy life focusing on career advancement, entertainment and sexual exploits is causing men to be passive both at home and in the church. Many of these men are identifying as Christians simply because they spend 1.5 hours a week at a local church service.

The standard for manhood has been lowered dramatically in our culture and churches. Jesus didn't die a gruesome death so that you could have your name on the member roster at a church you occasionally attend. Biblical manhood is a much higher calling. As King Solomon puts it in Psalms 127:1, "Unless the Lord builds the house, those who build it labor in vain. Unless the Lord watches over the city, the watchman stays awake in vain." These words are coming from one of the richest and wisest men the world had ever seen—a man who, as the Bible describes, had everything. And after all this, he says unless God is in control and guiding you, it's all pointless.

In 2007, when God allowed my (Tom Gensler) life to crumble around me, it brought me to the point of confessing, "I don't know what it means to be a godly man." He then sent me on a journey to discover the answer to my question. Among the many things I learned in those years, one of the most foundational was realizing how important it is to know your identity. You don't just need to know *who* you are; you need to know *whose* you are. If you have given your life to Jesus, you belong to Him. You are a child of God, created in His image. We are God's personal handiwork; the pinnacle of His creative act.

However, it will never be enough to simply know these truths in our heads. We must lay claim to this identity and hold it close to our hearts. You may be as tough as Jackie Sherrill and let an alligator take a chunk from your backside, but that is all secondary to your identity as a son.

So, do you have what it takes to lead other men deeper with God? The short answer is no, and we would say the majority of men would agree with these sentiments. Apart from Christ, none of us have what it takes to do *anything* good.

We are seeing, more than ever, that the men who move into the clergy are seminary graduates, or hold some sort of degree or certification from a Bible college. What this has indirectly taught men is that they need to have a degree in order to teach. Before we continue, hear me out: we are *not* saying that it is a bad thing to hire seminary-trained pastors, youth leaders, etc. However, what we are saying is that it has inadvertently made us feel that we need to defer to the training of others; to the "church professionals." When we see these types of people in leadership, it makes us feel unqualified and left behind.

> And because you are sons, God has sent the Spirit of His Son into our hearts, crying, 'Abba! Father!' So you are no longer a slave, but a son, and if a son, then an heir through God.
> – Galatians 4:6-7

So now we have the local church modeling that all the teaching should be left to the trained professionals, regardless of if that standard was set intentionally or not. A high percentage of men in the local church have never met with a more mature man and studied the Bible or developed a relationship. We are also seeing that the vast majority of men are not leading their homes the way that they were designed. We believe that this is again due to the belief that they need to have all the answers or training to be the spiritual head. They might even see their wives as more "spiritual" than them. The devil has gotten into their head and confirmed the lies they hear every day:

"You don't have what it takes."

"You are going to look stupid."

"Your wife is going to resist your leadership because you don't know enough."

When these lies are combined with a lack of understanding of what it looks like to invest in others, we find one of our greatest weaknesses: passivity. We relegate our responsibility to our wives, our pastors, and anyone else but us stepping up and leading courageously. Passivity is rearing its ugly head in men all around the world. Passivity's roots were born in the

Garden of Eden, when Eve was tempted by the serpent to eat from the tree of knowledge. If you read Genesis 3:6, you'll see where it says, "So when the women saw that the tree was good for food, and that it was a delight to the eyes, and that tree was to be desired to make one wise, she took of its fruit and ate, and she also gave some to her husband who was with her, and he ate." Adam was with Eve the entire time the serpent was tempting her, and he stood by and did nothing! This is passivity defined.

Men are standing by as our culture slips away into sin, our marriages fall apart around us, and our wives and women are forced to lead in roles they were not created for. Passivity is causing men to watch their children be raised by TV and video games, while fathers check out seeking pleasure and escape in sporting events and sinful activities on the internet like pornography and video gaming. Passivity carries over into the spiritual realm with men failing to lead in the most basic of tasks such as ushering and leading Sunday school classes.

It is staggering how many churches we have met with that share the same unfortunate truth: the pastor—the lead shepherd of the flock—has never been personally discipled by someone. Plain and simple, it is impossible to lead people somewhere you've never been. How should we expect to disciple other people if we've never been discipled ourselves? If you want other men to follow your example, you have to both be discipled and be discipling others.

Thankfully, we have also seen many pastors own this and humbly ask, "Can you help me?" We realize there is a great deal of pressure on pastors to preach, cast vision, and lead people. It is understandable that it is a challenge to set aside time to invest in someone one-on-one, or even in a small group. The reality is, if pastors are not investing in other men, yet tell their people to do it… that is the definition of hypocrisy. All of us who are parents know that if we tell our children to do (or not do) something, but we do the opposite, they are more likely to mimic our actions instead of listening to us. We have to walk the talk in order for people to truly listen.

* * *

Let's take it back to the question at the beginning of this section: "Do you think you have what it takes?"

No is the right answer in that on our own, we don't have what it takes. We are not able to walk the talk in our own strength. Truth is, if we had not been redeemed by Christ and filled with the Holy Spirit, we would never be qualified. Discipleship is only possible with the indwelling of the Holy Spirit and humble dependence on Christ. However, if we understand that we are in constant need of God's help, then we have what it takes to disciple others. Extraordinary things become possible when we submit our lives to the leading of God.

Those who would say yes to the question above have likely been poured into and had a correct understanding of discipleship. Just like Christ's original disciples, they have seen it modeled by someone else. They have had someone who helped them open God's word, apply it to their lives, pray, and develop spiritual disciplines. They are applying what Paul gives us in 2 Timothy 2:2: "…and what you have heard from me in the presence of many witnesses entrust to faithful men, who will be able to teach others also."

Again, these types of men are rare.

We believe the idea to "lower the bar" of discipleship is a good and right concept. However, when we say lower the bar, we are not saying dumb it down. Lowering the bar is the idea that every man, in every church, everywhere is capable of investing in the lives of other men. What we *are* saying is that Jesus gave all believers a direct command in His great commission in Matthew 28:18-20, "And Jesus came and said to them, 'All authority in heaven and on earth has been given to Me. Go therefore and make disciples of all the nations, baptizing them in the name of the Father, the Son and the Holy

Spirit, teaching them to observe all I have commanded you. And behold, I am with you always, to the end of the age."

This passage has been described as Jesus's last-minute command to his disciples. Jesus had already died and risen again and knew that his time on earth was nearing the end. His Father had given Him the authority and commission, and now He is giving it to us. Doesn't this sound just like discipleship? Jesus is teaching us to go forth and advance the Kingdom by teaching other people what we have been taught.

This command to make disciples is for every person that has placed their faith in Christ alone, not just for the professionals. The remaining disciples Jesus was speaking to weren't professionals—why should we expect that we need to be?

So, do you have what it takes? Yes, you do.

Still, the question remains: if we know we have what it takes, why aren't we all making disciples? Given the fact that the great commission is a command, not a suggestion, why are we not taking it seriously? This command is, in essence, what the church exists to carry out. The mission of every church should be to make disciples.

In James 4:17, he says, "So whoever knows the right thing to do and fails to do it, for him it is sin." This verse has challenged us greatly to be obedient to God's word. If what is right is to be "making disciples," and we do not do it, then it is sin. We must understand that sin is ultimately rebellion against God.

A big hindrance to making disciples is the fear of failure. You might be thinking, "What if I screw this person up? What if I tell them something unbiblical?" Isn't it true that we are bound to make mistakes when trying something new? You're not perfect. No one is. We aren't looking for perfection; we are looking for progress! You will make mistakes, but there is nothing that you can do to screw up the sovereignty of God. Trust that He will guide you, speak through you, and direct you. Though you may not know every answer to every question or understand every nuance in the Bible, God does, and He will make it clear to you.

The Christian life is much like the story of the Chinese Bamboo Tree. Like any plant, the growth of the Chinese Bamboo Tree requires nurturing: water, fertile soil, and sunshine. In its first year, there will be no visible signs of growth or activity. In its second, third, and fourth year of life, there is still no growth that is visible above the soil. However, like so many of us, the development is happening beneath the surface. It takes years of patience to continue to nurture something that is seemingly futile. On the fifth year of this plant's life, it grows 80 feet in just six weeks.

1 Corinthians 3:6-7 says, "I planted, Apollos watered, but God gave the growth. So neither he who plants nor he who waters is anything, but only God who gives the growth."

Though it might be easy to believe from what our eyes can see, this plant did not sit dormant for five years before it suddenly started growing. In fact, the growth was simply happening beneath the surface. Change was occurring; we just couldn't see it.

We believe there are many men in local churches all over America that are qualified; the Holy Spirit has been doing a great work in them, but no one could see it. Now, it is time for the growth to break through the soil and bear the fruit of what has been happening internally.

But still, there are others that may not be quite ready yet. There are likely two camps of men who are reading this book.

The first camp is men who are ready to be **disciple-makers**. You may already be investing in at least one other man with the desire to see both of you grow in the likeness of Christ.

The second camp is men who need to **be discipled**. You either already have or are aware of your need to have at least one other man investing in you for the purpose of looking more like Christ.

So, where do you start? Whom do you start with?

When we look at the life of Jesus, we see that it started in prayer. Before calling his disciples, he went to the mountain and prayed to His father.

Luke 6:12-13 says, "In these days he went out to the mountain to pray, and all night he continued in prayer to God. And when day came, he called his disciples and chose from them twelve, whom he named apostles."

Jesus is our model in everything, and everything we do should start in prayer. A good first step is to pray for God to show you where and with whom He wants you to start. Don't over-complicate it by overthinking. Just be open to what God might speak to you and how He might do it.

A good idea is to look at those already in your sphere of influence. If this is your first time considering discipling another man, then we highly recommend you begin sharpening your skills with your own family. Start with your wife and kids. Something we've learned about discipling our kids up in the faith is they have a tremendous amount of grace for us and like spending time with us. The Scriptures listed below will give you some starting points to begin this new journey:

Your Wife: Ephesians 5:25-26 says, "Husbands, love your wives, just as Christ also loved the church and gave Himself up for her, so that He might sanctify her, having cleansed her by the washing of water with the word."

Your Children: Ephesians 6:4 says, "Fathers, do not provoke your children to anger, but bring them up in the discipline and instruction of the Lord."

Faithful Men: 2 Timothy 2:2 says, "...and what you have heard from me in the presence of many witnesses, entrust these to faithful men who will be able to teach others also."

Again, we will say: do not over-complicate things! This should be fairly straightforward. Start in prayer, look around you, and go for it. Think about friends, neighbors, co-workers, and extended family.

A simple plan to follow:

1. Meet weekly
2. Get to know one another
3. Open Scripture
4. Apply them
5. Pray

We recommend you meet **weekly**. The bi-weekly and monthly meetings don't seem to gain traction. So much life happens in between your time together that you spend most of your time catching up. The first few weeks (and possibly months) can be spent **getting to know each other** in a real and intimate way. **Share Scripture** that is meaningful to you. **Apply Scripture** to life situations you may be talking about. Or, as you are sharing how you have dealt with difficulty in your life, bring those verses to mind that helped you. We like to always ask how can we **pray** for the man we are discipling. Our goal is to encourage and lift him up. Prayer is the best way to do that. Plus, it gives you things to think on and pray about in between your next meeting and allows you to begin your next time together with how the things that you agreed to pray about this past week are coming along.

Here is what we can promise by entering into a disciple-making relationship with other men: it will be challenging, and may get uncomfortable at times, but it will be good. It will stretch you both, and it will get messy, but it will grow your dependence and faith. Ultimately, it will honor God and bring Him the glory.

* * *

Who am I... a Disciple-maker or Disciple?

The exercise below is meant to help you identify if you should be a disciple-maker or a disciple. Put a checkmark by each question that describes yourself.

1. _____ I have surrendered my life to Christ and can clearly articulate the change/transformation that the Holy Spirit has been doing in my life.

2. _____ I consider myself honest, open, and transparent.

3. _____ I consider myself faithful, available, and teachable.

4. _____ I have a daily walk with the Lord. (In saying this, you are daily seeking God through His word and you are leading your family to the best of your ability to be more like Christ.)

5. _____ I have been discipled by other men; I have met with another man who was more spiritually mature, and he helped me develop spiritual disciplines that have produced measurable fruit in my life.

6. _____ I have been meeting with a group of godly men to develop relationships and be accountable. These men love me and regularly encourage and challenge me.

7. _____ I am a member in good standing with my local church and am actively involved. My pastor would say I could be counted upon as a leader who follows through with advancing the mission/vision of our church.

8. _____ I have put myself in a position where trusted church leaders have shared opportunities to grow. And the correction I received from them, I was able to apply to my life.

9. _____ I am married. We have weathered the storms of life together and stuck it out for God's glory.

10. _____ I have parented children who are living productive lives and have their own vibrant walk with the Lord.

11. _____ I have a career. I understand the difficulties of balancing work and home, and I intentionally bring God into my workplace.

12. _____ I have experienced sorrow, grief, and difficulty in this life and have purposefully chosen to follow Christ even more than before the trial.

The exercise above is our attempt at helping you determine if you are ready to be a disciple-maker, or if you should first seek a man to disciple you. This is not a foolproof way of determining if you are ready, rather just a way of asking you to assess yourself honestly. If you placed a checkmark by seven of the twelve questions, we encourage you to take what God has done in your life and share it with others. If you did not have seven checkmarks, this does not mean you are not ready; it simply suggests you find someone to help you grow in your relationship with the Lord.

We also suggest you ask a few other trusted men around you to honestly assess you. These men will need to have spent time with you before this assessment and know you fairly well. Ask them to read these twelve statements and see if they give you a similar score that you gave yourself.

There is no perfect Christian this side of heaven, but disciple-makers do need to be men who are yielding to the Spirit's leading and in submission to a local church and pastor. Disciple-makers should be men who see their marriage and family as top priorities, second only to their personal walk with God.

Before you think about investing in another man, make sure you are investing in your wife and children. We are certain your wife will respond very positively to you washing her with the word and praying with her. Your kids will love spending time with you, no matter their age. By teaching them what God is teaching you, they will have invaluable deposits to their spiritual bank account that will pay off for decades to come.

CHAPTER 4

How to Initiate Real-life Discipleship

THE NUMBER ONE QUESTION we are asked from pastors and men that we come in contact with is, "How do you disciple another man?" One of our primary reasons for writing this book is the number of men who have asked this question (not to mention those who have not asked).

Let us explain that last little bit. Most men don't ask because they let their pride get in the way. They are afraid to appear stupid or uninformed, so they don't come out and ask the question. Ironically, this fear points to their spiritual immaturity and lack of discipleship up until this point. Do you remember being in school and hearing almost every teacher say the same thing about questions? "There is no such thing as a stupid question. You never know if 15 other people in the class are wondering the same thing but are too afraid to ask."

This issue presents itself even more awkward for pastors and men who are mature in biblical knowledge and understanding. Now, hear us out: we would never say that if you haven't been in a discipleship relationship that you are immature. We know plenty of mature men who haven't experienced that level of discipleship. The reality is no seminary that we are aware of actually teaches pastors about discipleship. We also know by meeting with many pastors they have also never been discipled by another man.

* * *

As you may remember, we defined discipleship in chapter two: we would say discipleship is one man investing in one or more men by walking alongside those men on a regular basis. The same kind of relational discipleship that we see Jesus and countless other men in the Bible modeling for us; the same kind of relationship you can see being lived out in both the Old Testament and New Testament, men like David and Jonathan, Barnabus and Paul and Paul and Timothy.

Discipleship is messy, honest, open and transparent time spent with others. It involves confessing sin, forgiveness and fighting together with accountability. Most importantly, it is built on the foundation of reading and applying the truth of God's word in our lives.

Although we have made our case for it, we ultimately leave it open for you to wrestle with your own definition that most replicates Jesus' example of investing in a few other men. Whatever conclusion you come to, it is important to remember that biblical discipleship must be relational at its core. God the Father is relational, God the Son is relational, and God the Holy Spirit is relational. It is simply part of the beauty and mystery of the Trinity; three persons and one God declaring a Holy relationship. That means that if we are going to initiate real-life discipleship, we must enter into a relationship with others for the intent in maturing in Christ.

Unfortunately, many men see this task of going and making disciples much like Dorothy and her comrades in the Wizard of Oz. If you haven't seen it, there is a scene towards the end where she is standing in front of the Great Oz. His voice is booming and scary, and a distorted face takes over the screen. Smoke and fire are billowing up in front of Dorothy, causing her to shiver in fear. The Tin Man's knees are knocking, and the Lion is so scared he faints as Oz commands them to, "Bring me the broomstick of the wicked witch of the west!" Oz has just issued his great commission to Dorothy and her crew. Oz's command caused them fear and despair, and we are sure he wasn't expecting them to actually be successful.

With that in mind, we are confident that when Jesus gave us the Great Commission, He didn't intend for it to scare us, or with the expectation that we couldn't carry it out! Instead, He had shown the twelve (and us) what discipleship looked like by living it out in front of them for three years. He sent them out in pairs, showing them that revival happens in small communities of men. He showed them that discipleship was just to be a way of life with those God has placed around us. Jesus even promised to send us a Helper. Our lesson here is we can't do this on our own, but only by the power of the Holy Spirit in us.

Why do we always want to complicate something Jesus intended to be a regular part of our lifestyle?

It's sad to say we do so for a myriad of reasons: fear, pride, selfishness and ignorance, to name a few. We are sure you can compile your own list, but those are some of ours. We can also give Satan his props here too; he wants nothing more than to keep us in all those places that blockade us from carrying out the great commission. He wants us isolated and alone. He often presents himself and life's troubles as much larger than they really are. We refer to this as the peacock effect. He's not actually that large and intimidating, but in the midst of trials in our marriage, finances, and workplace, the enemy backs us down and puts us in our place of apathy and passivity.

By the grace of God, I (Tom Cheshire) was lucky to have men like Scott Brindley and James Talley, who modeled discipleship for me in a way that blew up all my excuses. How did they do it? They met with me regularly, asked me questions, listened and asked more questions. Most of all, they opened God's word and helped me to apply it. It was so easy and straightforward that I didn't even really understand what they were doing. They were simply living out 2 Timothy 2:2. They were investing the gospel in other men, so they, in turn, would go and invest in still more men. They had been discipled themselves, and they looked for who God was drawing near to them, whether it was at the workplace, church or a grocery store.

These men took the step to begin intentionally investing in another man. Was it scary? Yep! Was it good, and am I forever thankful for these men and their investment? Yep! Recognizing the need to multiply is the fruit of biblical discipleship. A step on the road to spiritual maturity is acknowledging that someone has taken the time to invest in me with what they have learned about life, God and manhood, and I now see the need to take their investment and multiply it in the life of others.

While there are many books out there that have developed complex plans and formulas to spiritual maturity, it doesn't *have to* be complicated. While we would agree there is some structure, planning and organization to discipleship, we would push back that they do not need to be complex. Simply put, Jesus' life of investing in the twelve was not complex or complicated. He just lived life day in and day out with them. In a word, it is a lifestyle. Though in some ways you are taught, like how to study the Bible or practical applications, discipleship is much more *caught* than taught. If you surround yourself with men who are doing what you want to be doing, you can't help but learn when you're around them. We have found that once you experience a healthy biblical model of Christ-like discipleship, you can't help but want to share it with others. It is merely imperfect men sharing how God's word is real and applying it, not trusting in our own abilities, but trusting in Christ and the Holy Spirit.

* * *

So how do we initiate this discipleship lifestyle?

Pray! Before Jesus selected the 12 disciples, he went up on the mountain and spent the night praying. Again, Jesus is our perfect model. He is the perfect disciple-maker! Pray, then watch for who God draws near to you. Keep your eyes open wherever you go. Who knows, you could run into someone at Home Depot. However, be warned—it may not be the type of man you thought it would be. It very well may, but you must be open to who God wants over who *you* want.

> **"** In these days he went out to the mountain to pray, and all night he continued in prayer to God. And when day came, he called his disciples and chose from them twelve, whom he named apostles. (Luke 6:12-13) **"**

Then, simply ask God for the courage to approach that man (or multiple men) with the simple question, "Would you like to start meeting with me?"

We see so many men that don't know how to start a relationship with another man. Most of the time, it is likely because we have never been on the receiving end of this conversation, so it feels awkward. But guess what? That's more than okay because it forces you to walk in humility. It forces you to be honest with that man that you don't really know what you are doing, but what you do know is that God has called you to make disciples. The rest we can just figure out as we go. Besides, men appreciate honesty and transparency, and if that is what we want to model, then what better way than from the beginning, right?

Let us encourage you, as you begin meeting up with guys, some will only need a little help and therefore, your time may be short lived. That's okay. Others may need or desire much more time and effort, and may last a year or more. That's okay too. The amount of time you spend meeting together isn't something we need to keep score of; rather we just need to be obedient and trust in the Holy Spirit, who is *the* change agent in us and others. As you do this, you will grow in maturity as well as helping others become more like Christ.

In Chapter 5, we will get into the real practical ways you build these relationships, so let's stay on track here and discuss some of the (many) reasons why real-life discipleship is messy.

REASON #1: It's a sacrifice.

Regardless of your schedule, profession, or season of life, it is a sacrifice for you and the men you disciple to meet. We all only get 24 hours in every day, which means you will have to give up some time every week. Don't let that be your excuse—you will always have time if you make time. The men you seek to meet with will have the same obstacle, so be ready to tackle that excuse together. If you are married and have children, it will mean sharing what you are doing with them so they are aware of the time commitment. Don't share the details of your time, but instead explain the call you see from God and His mandate to make disciples. Which, of course, should be lived out first with your wife and children. We would say that if by reading this book and stepping out in obedience to start investing in others leads you to leading your wife and children in spiritual growth, that alone would be a great win for advancing God's Kingdom here on earth!

Much like tithing and giving to other ministries, your first priority is home. Your sacrificial giving requires you to sacrifice splurging on that new motorcycle, clothes, or watch so that you can invest in other ministries. The same principle exists in discipleship: you will need to sacrifice the time you might want to spend doing some other things to be able to invest in the men God has placed in your life.

More importantly, if this conversation with your wife and kids reveals you need to invest in them, and now is not the season to be investing outside of your home, then that is a win for Christ and the Kingdom. Remember how we started this process? Pray! Listen to God as you pray and ask Him to show you how well you are investing in your marriage and family. Be obedient to that answer above all. Quite honestly, it was by investing in our wife and kids' spiritual health that we became a much more effective disciple-maker outside our homes.

Remember, this is not about perfection. Our marriages will never be perfect, nor will our families ever be perfect, but both of those should be on solid footing before we venture outside the home to make disciples. Our disciple-making will not be perfect, either! Discipleship, like spiritual maturity is not about perfection; it's about progress. Progress in Christ-likeness. God's grace is sufficient, even in this.

REASON #2: Not everyone is like you.

We all have unique personalities, quirks, and character traits that make us who we are. That means you are likely very different than the men you will be in relationship with. It will be important to have a grasp on your strengths and weaknesses, personality (i.e., introvert or extrovert, timid or assertive, etc.) how God has wired you, and your unique spiritual giftedness. As you understand yourself more fully, it will help you to understand others—both those who might be very similar to you and those who are your polar opposite in every way.

In my case, Scott Brindley helped me (Tom Cheshire) to truly understand grace. He has the ability to see the best in everybody he comes in contact with. No matter what their background, or what sin they are currently struggling with, he can extend grace just like Jesus. I, on the other hand, am pretty legalistic. I am a black and white thinker, and it's hard for me to extend grace not only to others but to myself as well. Scott didn't beat me up and point out my lack of grace, though he very well could have! Instead, he used real-life circumstances to show me how one extends grace—first, by extending it to me, and then showing me how he extended it to others. He pointed me to Scriptures like Ephesians 2:5, Romans 5:8-10, and Ephesians 2:8-9 (if you're a poor grace-giver like me, I encourage you to look them up as well).

Over the years, I have also been discipled by men who are wired more like me. The similarities in personality allowed me to see myself in their stories. For example, their testimonies of how God revealed their selfishness and later delivered them made perfect sense to me—one who wrestles with selfishness often.

In the end, know that your personality and those of the men God would draw near to you will be all over the spectrum. The differences will create healthy tension, including opportunities to confess, repent and ask for forgiveness. If we are called to sharpen one another as iron sharpens iron, that will likely create some uncomfortable friction, don't you think? But, ultimately, the tension will shape you to be more like Christ, which will impact your marriage, your family, and your witness.

REASON #3: There are five types of men within the local church.

The last obstacle we'll talk through is what we call *the five types of men within the local church*. Over the course of our ministry experience, we've determined that as you begin looking around the landscape of your church, there are five types of men you will come across. Much like understanding the way you're wired, knowing the condition and types of men you're dealing with will allow you to understand others as you encounter them. Before you analyze others, you'll need to identify which group you are in.

We have the:

- The Nowhere Man (lost)
- The Around Man (immature)
- The Regular Man (maturing)
- The Gets It Man (leader/mature)
- The Hurting man (any of the above)

The Nowhere Man is as described above… he's lost! Most likely, the Nowhere Man is not often seen at church. In fact, he may never come, but you know of him because his wife and kids are regular attendees. This man could be the one you work with, your neighbor, or maybe even a family member. This man doesn't see much relevancy with the church. There is a high probability that he has had negative experiences with the local church throughout his life,

> **For the word of the cross is folly to those who are perishing...**
> – 1 Corinthians 1:18

which have led him to conclude that he doesn't need it. You need to be praying for these men that, as Jesus is quoted as saying to the Apostle Paul in Acts 26:18, "...that their eyes will be opened, so that they may turn from darkness to light and from the power of Satan to God, that they may receive forgiveness of sins and place among those who are sanctified by faith in me." This man requires us to be gracious in our approach, and he requires us to be winsome with the gospel. He needs to hear our testimony of how Christ rescued us—how we are a sinner saved by grace and being sanctified in that same grace.

The Around Man is coming to church, but not regularly. He hasn't made a serious commitment to God or his local church. However, we believe that the Holy Spirit is at work in this man, and he is beginning to make the connection that God needs to become much greater in his life than he is now. John 6:44 says, "No one can come to me unless the Father who sent me draws him." This man needs you to notice him! He needs to know you care about his soul more than you care about giving him something to do. We believe this guy is open and ready for the next step. He needs a man like you to invite him. Maybe it's an invite to a men's gathering held by your church, or maybe it's an invite to a Christian men's conference. The Around Man is likely making the connection that God needs to be a significant point in his life.

The Regular Man is just that—he's regular. This guy is most likely seen with his family at everything the church hosts. He has seen the connection with Scripture and the application to his life. Luke 24:25 says, "Then he opened their minds to understand the Scriptures." This man understands that his local church and his relationships with other men are important and helpful to his life. He understands his inability to do these things through his own power, and that he needs God to do things through him. Proverbs 16:9 says, "The heart of a man plans his way, but the Lord establishes his steps." The Regular Man is open to meeting with other men and invites them to speak into his life. He is starting to see the gifts and talents that God has given him to use for the benefit of others and the advancement of God's kingdom.

The Gets It Man is what the title implies: He understands that God has a unique plan for his life and that he needs to live and act like a mature man of God. 1 Corinthians 13:11 says, "When I was a child, I spoke like a child, I thought like a child, I reasoned like a child. When I became a man, I gave up childish ways." This man is investing in others because others have invested him (2 Timothy 2:2). He understands giving grace because much grace has been given to him (2 Corinthians 12:9). He considers others more important than himself (Philippians 2:3). He is asking how he can serve within his local church and community. He has transitioned from using language like "what can I get out of this," to using language such as "how can I serve and help others with my time, talent, and resources."

The Hurting Man can be in any of these categories. Life has put him in a hard place. He may not have ever known the Lord. If that's the case, then the gospel can be presented to save him. 1 Timothy 2:3-4 says, "God our Savior, who desires all men to be saved and to come to the knowledge of the truth." If he is in the Around, Regular, or Gets It categories, but is hurt, then he needs you to love him and help guide him. The Hurting Man needs to see how God's grace is the balm to soothe his pain. He needs to understand that there is nothing he is experiencing that Jesus can't relate to with him. He needs to know that, "Since then we have a great high priest who has passed through the heavens, Jesus, the Son of God, let us hold fast our confession. For we do not have a high priest who is unable to sympathize with our weaknesses, but one who in every respect has been tempted as we are, yet without sin. Let us then with confidence draw near to the throne of grace, that we may receive mercy and find grace to help in time of need." (Hebrews 4:14-16)

We have described to you the five different types of guys you are going to encounter in your church. Each of them will present different challenges as you engage and seek to invest in helping them take steps closer to Christ. Please understand that all these relationships are going to take time. As we have mentioned, some will take more time than others. Begin looking at discipleship as a lifelong commitment of sorts, in that there is no shortcut or fast track. There is no "Discipleship for Dummies" book with three easy steps to maturity.

Think of discipleship as spiritual parenting. If you have children, especially adult children, you know that you never stop *being* their parent. Your involvement and influence change, as well as your communication and techniques, but you are always going to be their parent. That will never change. What we are saying is that even though you may not always be in a formal discipleship relationship for your entire lives, you will likely be in contact for much longer than your initial discipleship commitment. Every relationship is different, and every relationship will take a different amount of time.

If we go into this thing with our eyes wide open, knowing that commitment and sacrifice is a lifestyle, and life will have its highs and lows, we stand a much better chance of enduring for the sake of the Gospel. On the contrary, if we go in thinking that this will be easy, quick and painless, we'll likely want to quit the moment things get a little rocky.

Here are a few passages of Scripture we suggest pondering and studying when it comes to discipleship. The Apostle Paul makes it very clear that the entire life of a Christian is one of endurance, not just in the area of making disciples. Furthermore, our accolades or accomplishments (or how many men we are discipling) are not to be celebrated so we can make much of us, but so we can make much of Christ.

Read 1 Corinthians 9:20-27: "To the Jews I became as a Jew, in order to win Jews. To those under the law I became as one under the law (though not being myself under the law) that I might win those under the law. To those outside the law I became as one outside the law (not being outside the law of God but under the law of Christ) that I might win those outside the law. To the weak I became weak, that I might win the weak. I have become all things to all people, that by all means I might save some. I do it all for the sake of the gospel, that I may share with them in its blessings. Do you not know that in a race all the runners run, but only one receives the prize? So run that you may obtain it. Every athlete exercises self-control in all things. They do it to receive a perishable wreath, but we an imperishable. So I do not run aimlessly; I do not box as one beating the air. But I discipline my body and keep it under control, lest after preaching to others I myself should be disqualified."

Philippians 3:12-14: "Not that I have already obtained this or am already perfect, but I press on to make it my own, because Christ Jesus has made me his own. Brothers, I do not consider that I have made it my own. But one thing I do: forgetting what lies behind and straining forward to what lies ahead, I press on toward the goal for the prize of the upward call of God in Christ Jesus."

2 Timothy 4:1-8: "I charge you in the presence of God and of Christ Jesus, who is to judge the living and the dead, and by his appearing and his kingdom: preach the word; be ready in season and out of season; reprove, rebuke, and exhort, with complete patience and teaching. For the time is coming when people will not endure sound teaching, but having itching ears they will accumulate for themselves teachers to suit their own passions, and will turn away from listening to the truth and wander off into myths. As for you,

always be sober-minded, endure suffering, do the work of an evangelist, fulfill your ministry. For I am already being poured out as a drink offering, and the time of my departure has come. I have fought the good fight, I have finished the race, I have kept the faith. Henceforth there is laid up for me the crown of righteousness, which the Lord, the righteous judge, will award to me on that day, and not only to me but also to all who have loved his appearing."

> And whatever you do, in word or deed, do everything in the name of Lord Jesus, giving thanks to God the Father through Him.
> – Colossians 3:17

Men, be encouraged that we live this life for Christ and the eternal reward, not for the earthly affirmation of men. We have one purpose from God, and that is to glorify Him in all we do.

See you in the very practical application in the next chapter.

CHAPTER 5

Launching

WE HAVE INTENTIONALLY KEPT this book short and simple to accomplish what we feel is lacking in our local churches: biblical, real-life discipleship. We wanted to produce something every man could read and understand that would launch them out into actual application. We desire that this book would be an effective tool in making disciple-makers. There are plenty of other books that spin men off into becoming process engineers. Discipleship is not something that should be complicated, but somehow, it has become just that. The idea of writing a book that was to the point has been our goal since the beginning—two regular guys who are attempting to faithfully follow our Lord Jesus Christ each and every day, sharing with you how God has impressed on us to fulfill his great commission to go and make disciples.

As a form of recap, let's go back and remember what we've covered thus far. In Chapter One, we shared our stories of how God used other men to completely change our lives. In Chapter Two, we gave you a clear definition of what discipleship is, and what it is not. In Chapter Three, we assured you that despite what the enemy might be saying to you, you have what it takes to invest in other men spiritually. In Chapter Four, we gave you some practical ways to connect and engage with another man to start a disciple-making relationship.

Now, we are going to give you some "rails to run on"—a sort of start-up kit, if you will. A piece of advice we most often give to pastors and men is, "Do *not* overthink this."

When I (Tom Cheshire) was a 12-year-old boy, I remember one of our neighbors being this "super-smart" electrical engineer. One day, I noticed he was working on his lawnmower, so I walked up and asked him what the problem was.

"I just can't get it started, no matter what I try. I've completely disassembled the engine, changed the spark plug and cleaned all the parts, put it back together, and it still won't start!" he said, exasperated.

I gave it a couple pulls myself to see, and nothing happened. "Does it have gas in it?" I asked, thinking it couldn't be that easy. I was wrong. He took the gas cap off and looked in the tank… no gas. He sheepishly put gas in it, and it promptly started and ran on the second pull.

Sometimes we are just like my neighbor when it comes to discipleship—we overthink it entirely. The core of real-life biblical discipleship is simple: establishing a relationship with other men. This really is as easy as getting to know each other. You don't need a curriculum or personality tests to get the motor running. We just need to put some gas in the tank and get started!

In order to paint a clear picture for you as to what discipleship should look like, two book titles come to mind. To be a disciple-maker, you must possess both of these characteristics if you are going to effective. Both were written by men we greatly admire; one we know personally, and the other only from afar. The first is by John Piper, who we have heard speak and read a lot of his books, but don't know personally. His book is called *Velvet Steel*, and is about a series of poems written for his wife during the first 42 years of their relationship, starting with the day of their engagement. He provides readers with a taste of one man's tender affections for his wife that he hopes will fan into flame readers affections for their own spouses, and ultimately for a deeper, more intimate relationship with God. Stu Weber's book, titled *Tender Warrior,* is exactly as the title suggests—teaching men to be the "tender warrior" that God desires for him and his family. A man that remains vigilant, but with the love and gentleness that is only found in a life yielded to Christ. Biblical discipleship requires toughness and tenderness; it requires a velvety exterior with a tough interior.

If we go back to our perfect model, Jesus, we can see that He exemplified these characteristics. It's no coincidence that in John 13:35, where Jesus practically shows the disciples what it means to be a servant leader, says, "By this all people will know that you are my disciples, if you have love for one another." We know there was a dispute among the disciples as to who was the greatest, and while there are many lessons taught in the upper room discourse of John 13-17, Chapter 13 makes it clear that to be "great" means you must serve more than you are served. It's as if Jesus was saying, "Gentlemen, discipleship is going to require you to think less about yourself and more about others. It is actually going to cost you, and one of those costs is going to be time." Jesus had been talking with them throughout his time with them, and now he was showing them what He had been talking so much about. The King was going to wash their feet—the task set aside for the lowliest of the low was now taken on by the Most High. Jesus' example exemplifies a tender warrior; a man of velvet *and* steel.

After a number of years discipling men, I (Tom Gensler) was still experiencing limited success—meaning the men I was investing in seemed to bear very little good, biblical fruit. Shortly after I realized my lack of "success," I had an encounter with the Holy Spirit in my quiet time that changed me. The Lord revealed to me that I was trying to do his job; I was trying to be the one to change their hearts and lives when He was the only one fit for that kind of work. God kindly showed me that I was not doing a very good job at it anyway. He then shared that my role was to be a lover and encourager to the men and leave the rest up to Him.

God said, "Tom, you need to be the conduit to help connect the men to Me and My word, and I will take it from there."

From that point forward, I was able to see things differently. I see love as the benchmark. In fact, I would summarize that much of what you need to be doing for the men God sends your way is to love them.

Have you ever thought about what Jesus endured while discipling his twelve men? The fact that Jesus spent 3 years, 24 hours a day, 7 days a week with his twelve is astounding. Here is a short "highlight" reel of some of the more challenging memories.

He sent them out two-by-two, and they all failed their first practical application. James and John were confused about Jesus' mission on earth, and started arguing over who was going to be greater in the Kingdom to come. Then, Judas flat-out betrayed him. As Jesus was preparing for the cross, he asked for his closest friends to join him in prayer, and he finds them sleeping instead. Peter, his main guy, not only denied knowing Jesus when He was arrested, but denied it three separate times! Can you imagine how this must have felt?

The theme woven throughout the gospels of Jesus is love. The passage that captures the deep essences of Jesus' love is found in John 21:15-18, "When they had finished breakfast, Jesus said to Simon Peter, 'Simon, son of John, do you love me more than these?' He said to him, 'Yes, Lord; you know that I love you.' He said to him, 'Feed my lambs.' He said to him a second time, 'Simon, son of John, do you love me?' He said to him, 'Yes, Lord; you know that I love you.' He said to him, 'Tend my sheep.' He said to him the third time, 'Simon, son of John, do you love me?' Peter was grieved because he said to him the third time, 'Do you love me?' and he said to him, 'Lord, you know everything; you know that I love you.' Jesus said to him, 'Feed my sheep.'"

Jesus chose ordinary men who were working ordinary jobs to take his message to a lost world. He had remarkable insight to see what these men could be with His Spirit living inside of them. Jesus not only chose and loved those that others would have most certainly overlooked, but these were the same men that he was planning to commission to go and flip the world upside down. They were the least likely.

Remember, love should be our benchmark as we disciple. I (Tom Cheshire) look back on the men who discipled me, and they showed me an actual life lived out in love. First, with their love of Christ, then with their love for others, which included me. They loved me in all my sin, personality flaws, weaknesses, stupidity and selfishness. I am certain there were days that they had to press deep into Christ to keep from walking away... or physically accosting me! You see, Scott Brindley didn't ever tell me I needed to have more grace, he simply *showed me* grace time and time again. Scott lived that out with me. I grew to understand the grace of God through the grace of other men, and I was then challenged to be patient and love younger, less mature men just like they had done for me. Then, I turned around and exercised said grace and patience for others—specifically Tom Gensler—as I walked alongside him in the early years of our disciple-making relationship. I think Tom has grown immensely because of it, and now is better at extending grace and patience with the men that *he* is investing in.

We have tried to be as real and transparent as we can in this book to give you a glimpse of reality from our perspective. That's precisely why we must also talk about failure.

What? Failure? How can that be? After all, aren't we being obedient to Scripture and seeking to honor God? Why would God let us fail? Doesn't he know how hard this is?

Well, all it takes is reading your Bible from Genesis through Revelation to quickly see there are hundreds of stories that are ripe with failure. Let's look at the example of King David. David is one of the central figures of the entire Bible. He fought Goliath with a sling and stone and won, he demonstrated the kind of friendship men should have in his relationship with Jonathan, he taught us the model of worship in the book of Psalms, and showed us how to deal with a mean and difficult person like King Saul. It's hard to believe that King David, who is often spoken so highly of in Scripture, is guilty of breaking half of God's commandments. He coveted another man's wife (2 Samuel 11:2-3), he committed adultery with her (2 Samuel 11:4), he stole her from him (2 Samuel 12:9), he lied about it (2 Samuel 11:12-13), and then had her husband murdered (2 Samuel 12:9). This is just *one* story!

Failure is ripe in the life of Bible characters. However, David's story also demonstrates that when we have sinned, we must accept responsibility and ask for forgiveness. God can and is willing to use us still. The theme that is played out time and time again is this: failure humbled the person, creating a deeper dependence on God, and in most cases, it ultimately led to God's glory. Their failure was used by God to bring Him glory. Think about that.

We shouldn't go into real-life discipleship and think we are going to be the exception. There will be successes on some level that we see immediately; however, I suspect that ultimate eternal rewards will be ours as we see what we may have thought initially as a failure, was actually a step in a man's process to see his need for the grace that only Christ and the Gospel can deliver. We should be encouraged if we have, let's say, a 20% success rate of investing. That's to say two out of ten men go on to bear good fruit. If these two men go on to invest in other men, there will be souls saved, families redeemed and generations impacted. This 20% is

> ❝ As for that in the good soil, they are those who, hearing the word, hold it fast in an honest and good heart, and bear fruit with patience.
> – Luke 8:15 ❞

speculation as we haven't kept score of the men we have discipled, but we have seen men walk away from the faith. We only need to look at the gospels to read the parable of the sower, and see Jesus explains that only 25% of those will land in good soil and bear fruit.

Let me share two real-life stores with you of success and failure. I (Tom Cheshire) had a dear friend who acted on sin in such a way that his wife was crushed and hurt deeply. Not wanting to divorce or walk away from the marriage, she reached out to me and asked if I could meet with them. I sat with them as my friend confessed his sin, owned it and apologized. He professed his love for her and his desire to heal the marriage and regain her trust. Tears flowed from all of us; it was a very tender, incredible moment. My friend and I agreed right there in front of his wife to meet weekly, open God's word, confess, repent and have open accountability. We committed to asking hard questions and praying for wisdom. We also agreed that I would call his wife to check in and ask what she was seeing and experiencing to make sure we were all tracking together.

We met every week, opening the word and talking honestly. I would check in with his wife, and she would share how he was leading and loving his family. When he wasn't doing so well, she was open about that as well. Success, right? Wrong! We met for just about a year before I got another call from his wife. She was on the other line, sobbing profusely and screaming, "He's done it again!"

Neither of us knew when he started up his "secret" life again because he was posing—playing the game of husband and friend. He looked the part of a Christian husband and friend on the outside but was living a lie on the inside. His previous confession, and what appeared to be sincere repentance, was actually not. At some point, he began lying to both his wife and me once again. He was a poser, just like the Pharisees Jesus confronts in Matthew 23:27-28 "Woe to you, scribes and Pharisees, hypocrites! For you are like whitewashed tombs, which outwardly appear beautiful, but within are full of dead people's bones and all uncleanness. So you also outwardly appear righteous to others, but within you are full of hypocrisy and lawlessness."

Unfortunately, this man walked away from a marriage and family for his selfish desires, no matter how hard others had tried to love him.

I (Tom Cheshire) have been in many discipleship relationships with men over the last 20 years, and many have gone on to mature and continue discipling others. However, the reality is many have seemed to fall off the wagon—maybe not as bad as my friend in the story above, but by the looks of things, they aren't going on to love others. On the other hand, one of the examples I can point to came to me by way of asking a young man who had started coming to my church who had discipled him.

To my great surprise, he shared that it was a young man named David Lasley. I had invested in David for a couple of years, and our season reached an end in a right and healthy way. I knew David was actively serving in a local campus ministry, but we had lost touch. When the young man told me it was David who had discipled him, I am not going to lie; my heart leaped with joy and satisfaction! At the time, David was on staff as one of the male leaders of a college ministry called Christian Student Fellowship (CSF) at the University of Illinois at Springfield.

About five years earlier, David had sought me out and asked me if I would invest in him. I had first met David years before when our daughters were a part of CSF at the University of Illinois at Springfield, and David was one of the student leaders. When he approached me, he and his wife had just come on staff with CSF. He was newly married, and they had just had their first baby. We met weekly and opened God's word and talked about being a godly husband, loving his wife and being a good father. We talked through life and all of its challenges. I also tried to show David what it looked like to be a disciple-maker; to be a leader that invested in other young men to help them become godly men at the college level. David was also attending seminary to get his Master of Divinity Degree. We reached a point where we both agreed we could stop meeting and use that time to invest in others. The young man I met above is one of those men David invested in.

Success! David is one of my 20%.

* * *

As we wrap up this book, let us give you this encouragement: If you are reading this and have never been discipled, or have never discipled another man, be encouraged that both are possible for you. If you desire to be discipled, pray for boldness and courage to seek out a man you see in your church who you know has navigated life with Christ as a man, husband and father. If you are a man who desires to invest in the sacrificial service of other men, start with prayer. Pray for God to open your eyes to who you might commit to in your church. Know the following to be true: you will grow exponentially in your maturity as you love and invest in others.

As we've shared before, if you are married, we would encourage you that home is your starting ground. You must love and invest in your wife and children, as that is your first ministry. If you are doing that well and have the margin to invest in someone inside your church, then start praying. Pray as to who that would be, then trust in God and ask that man to join you. Remember Jesus' word to His disciples in Matthew 9:37-38 "Then he said to his disciples, 'The harvest is plentiful, but the laborers are few; therefore pray earnestly to the Lord of the harvest to send out laborers into his harvest.'"

We have wrestled with how formal of a commitment discipleship needs to be, and we can't give you a straight answer. Do you need to craft up an agreement for both parties? We would say, probably not. However, we would say there does need to be some sort of written expectations on your part to be given to the men you are discipling. But, that being said, there still needs to be room for flexibility and adaptation. Your personality and the personality of the man will somewhat dictate how the arrangement will best thrive for the mutual benefit of both and the glory of God.

Thank you for reading our book. We are praying for you! We desire this book to be a resource that propels you forward to make intentional investments in those around you. We pray that you see the biblical command and heart of God in loving others through discipleship. There is a sea full of men within the local church and our communities that need men like you to walk alongside them and teach them what you have learned about life. Discipleship can be slow, and you can become easily discouraged. Stay strong, be encouraged in the Lord, and hold fast to the words of John Newton: "Remember, the growth of a believer is not like a mushroom—but like an oak, which increases slowly indeed—but surely. Many suns, showers, and frosts, pass upon it before it comes to perfection. And in winter, when it seems to be dead—it is gathering strength at the root. Be humble, watchful, and diligent in the means, and endeavor to look through all, and fix your eyes upon Jesus and all shall be well."

We believe God desires men like you to run the race well. Whether it is investing in your wife and children, or others in your church, this book is the first step in moving from disciple to disciple-maker!

> " So if there is any encouragement in Christ, any comfort from love, any participation in the Spirit, any affection and sympathy, complete my joy by being of the same mind, having the same love, being in full accord and of one mind. Do nothing from selfish ambition or conceit, but in humility count others more significant than yourselves. Let each of you look not only to his own interests, but also to the interests of others. "
> – Philippians 2:1-4

CHAPTER 6

Sneak Peek of the Real-Life Discipleship Guide

O VER THE YEARS, WE HAVE shared a discipleship guide that has given men a framework for discipleship. However, most of the men we have shared this document with only needed 4-6 weeks of help to get started, and then they set off on their own. The other thing we noticed as we shared the document was the response from the men, time and time again:

"This is really simple!"

"Is this all there is to it?!"

Our response to them would be a resounding, "Yes! It really is that simple!"

As you read through the 6-week plan we provided here for you, you'll see that it really is just getting to know one another. As you get to know each other, and the more detail you can give and receive, the quicker the relationship will go deep.

If you find our framework helpful and want more, we have the rest of the entire Real-Life Discipleship Guide on our website for free. The choice is up to you on how to use them to your advantage. You can tweak them and make them your own, and you can use the same framework over and over again with different relationships.

Our desire in writing this book is to help normal, everyday men start investing in other men. We are not perfect; there is no such man except for Jesus. Discipleship is not about perfection, but it *is* about progress—progress in becoming more like Christ. What we are is *real men*, dealing with real-life and using Scripture to guide us to be more like Christ. If just 20% of the men who read this book go on to invest and be invested in by loving others, then we will celebrate with millions in heaven that God used them to make a difference for His Kingdom.

What follows is a sample of the Real-Life Discipleship Guide that can be downloaded for free on our website, www.rpmfm.org

Real-Life Discipleship Guide

Battle Proven

"No short cut exists for a deeper spiritual life... the man who would know God must give time to him."
- A.W. Tozer

For a free and complete download of the entire Real-Life Discipleship Guide, please visit www.rpmfm.org

Use passcode: RPMRLDG

Table of Contents

Section One: Spiritual Formation

- Build The Relationship

- Share Your Faith

- Why We Are Here

- Developing Spiritual Disciplines

- Understanding And Reading The Bible With A Plan

- Pray With A Purpose

- Build The Team

- Worshipping God

- Servant Leadership Within The Body Of Christ

- Fruit Of The Spirit

- Share What Christ Has Done In Your Life

- Develop A Game Plan For Spiritual Growth
- Take A Break And Journal About Your Marriage

Section Two: The Marriage Relationship

- Gods Design For Marriage
- Servant Leadership In Marriage
- Christ As The Example Of Servant Leadership
- Roles In Marriage
- Expectations From Your Wife And Meeting Her Needs
- Knowing Your Wives Love Language
- Communication And Conflict
- Sex And Pornography
- Develop A Game Plan To Honor God In Your Marriage
- Take A Break And Date Your Wife

Section Three: Family And Your Children

- What Kind Of Dad Do You Want to Be
- Successful Fathering
- What Your Children Need From You

- Develop A Plan For Fathering
- Take A Break And Date Your Children

Section Four: The Local Church And Your Manhood

- How Do You Fit Into Your Local Church
- Being Part Of The Solution
- Becoming A Servant In Your Local Church
- Develop A Game Plan To Compliment Your Pastor And Strengthen Your Church
- Take A Break And Meet With Your Pastor

Section Five: Your Career And Its Impact

- Your View Of Work
- Gods View Of Work
- Taking Christ Into The Workplace
- Your Manhood And Work
- Your Financial Stewardship
- Develop A Game Plan To Win At Work And Home
- Take A Break And Review Your Finances With Your Wife

Section Six: Working A Sustainable Game Plan

- Revisit Your Game Plan For Spiritual Disciplines
- Revisit Your Game Plan To Create Lasting Love In Your Marriage
- Revisit Your Game Plan To Invest In Your Children So They May Walk With Jesus Christ
- Revisit Your Game Plan To Serve Your Local Church
- Revisit Your Game Plan To Be A Man Of God At Work
- Take A Break Fast And Pray

Section Seven: Where Do We Go From Here

- How's It Working
- Roles Reversed
- Discuss Who's Next
- How Do You Become a Multiplier
- Passing The Baton Of Real-Life Discipleship
- Watch Me As I Lead

How to Use This Guide

The following pages are meant to be a guide providing you a topic, a scripture prompt to reflect on and help direct your conversation, and a set of example questions to help focus your conversation and time. There is a Godly purpose for each section and conversation. There are times built in for rest, with each section having a specific purpose.

As godly men, we need to live our lives ordered by priorities, and this guide follows the way we strive to live our lives in Him.

- **Section One** is all about deepening your relationship with God
- **Section Two** is about strengthening your marriage
- **Section Three** is about being the best father possible
- **Section Four** is about your interaction in your local church
- **Section Five** is how you take your faith into the workplace
- **Section Six** is revisiting your plans for growth in these areas

- **Section Seven** is developing a plan to multiply and impact more men

This guide will not provide answers to every question. But, you are a man committed to advancing the kingdom of God, so be assured: when mistakes happen and failures occur, God's grace is sufficient for you. So press on, trust in Christ, do your best and invest in other men as other men invest in you.

"What does it look like to disciple another man?"

MEN HAVE PONDERED THIS question for decades. They are wanting to help another man grow spiritually, yet have stopped short of becoming involved in disciple-making relationships because of fear of rejection, as well as not knowing what to do or where to start. This is not an exhaustive study on discipleship. Pastors and church leaders are often frustrated by the many offers of curriculums and resources that claim to help answer the question of "how to" disciple. Yet, in our experience, many give great information on why we should be discipling but fail to explain *how*. This is a practical guide to help the men of your church grow in Christ together and achieve the greater potential that God has for them. With the help of the Holy Spirit and our step-by-step approach on relevant topics, you will gain the know-how to achieve success and build godly relationships with the men of your local church.

We have personally witnessed the development of men who are better able to support their pastors and church leaders and strengthen their local church. Through the years, we were discipled by many godly men. This guide is the result of what was learned through the Holy Spirit and those God-inspired men.

> "...and what you have heard from me in the presence of many witnesses entrust to faithful men, who will be able to teach others also."
> – 2 Timothy 2:2

Discipleship is not easy, and going the distance requires much perseverance. However, if you commit to digging deep together, you will sharpen each other, and your lives will be examples to lead others on this journey as well.

God bless you. Know that we are praying for you.

Sincerely,

Tom Cheshire & Tom Gensler

Why Discipleship?

Christ followers should be disciples... this we know. The biblical model for Christ-likeness is investing in men one-on-one in their day-to-day living. The great commission Matthew 28:18-20 gives us the command to make disciples.

Think about this for a moment: imagine a corporate CEO having employees unclear of what's expected of them. Every employer we have ever had, first indoctrinated us on the details of the company, safety concerns, and the how-to and goals of our employment to ensure the company success, as well as ours. Our first few weeks were spent close to someone assigned to train and mentor us. Secular businesses spend vast amounts of resources training employees. If this works for corporate America, why can't we apply this same principle in our churches?

We're taught discipleship from church podiums, and monthly men's breakfasts turn out about a dozen participants; however, this is not discipleship training. This has been largely ineffective to train leaders on the nuts and bolts in the how-to of mentoring men. We're producing pew-sitters who hear a great message, are entertained and feel good, then leave thinking they have fulfilled their Christian moral obligation for the week.

Just as a seasoned employee of a secular company takes the new employee under their wing, ensuring their success in the company, men of God need other men of God to become godly men. We also believe women need women to speak into them to understand biblical womanhood. Granted, small group ministries have had a more significant impact than the weekly messages from the podium, but this is still not the biblical model.

Discipleship is relational, life-on-life; a more mature person getting together with another on a regular basis to develop a relationship, exchanging information to the benefit of both, developing and growing in spiritual maturity. We contend for applying the Christ-model of growing in relationship with other men, speaking the Word of God into each other's lives, and deepening each other's practical application of the gospel in all of life's situations as Christ did with His chosen few. We believe that this is the right approach. Jesus selected twelve men with whom He spent quality one-on-one time; three with whom he dedicated much more personal time, and one

> " Iron sharpens iron, and one man sharpens another.
> – Proverbs 27:17 "

particularly intimately. This is what we believe is the biblical model for discipleship.

> 66 Older men are to be sober-minded, dignified, self-controlled, sound in faith, in love, and in steadfastness. Older women likewise are to be reverent in behavior, not slanderers or slaves to much wine. They are to teach what is good, and so train the young women to love their husbands and children, to be self-controlled, pure, working at home, kind, and submissive to their own husbands, that the word of God may not be reviled. 99
> – Titus 2:2-5

Our focus is on discipling men. A man following God. A man who knows Him intimately and is becoming more Christ-like. A man who has a marriage and family, who has a genuine love and respect for his wife and wants to see his children become all that God wants them to be. A man who recognizes that his number one ministry is leading his wife and children closer to Christ, and does it each and every day—while going to work and working hard, demonstrating godly integrity and faith in Christ daily.

So, where are these men?

They're out there, but in limited numbers. Our heart's desire is to see armies of authentic gospel-centered men. We wake up every day desiring to see layers of discipleship taking place in local churches across America. By "layers" we mean that every man has a man discipling him, creating multi-generational investments in each other, all for the glory of Jesus Christ. Biblical manhood is in a state of confusion. For several generations, men have not had a clear vision of what biblical manhood looks like.

This is a guide intended to provide you with a relevant, practical, step-by-step approach to get involved in relationship with other men. This is *not* an exhaustive study on discipleship. There are plenty of resources available on this topic.

Discipleship is messy. Following this guide will likely also be messy, confusing at times, and difficult. You will be challenged. Turning away will sometimes seem like your best option, but you must resist those temptations. Christ called you to make disciples, and there are plenty of men who desperately want and need to be discipled. They don't act it, though. Just like us, they put on their church-face, but deep down, all followers of Jesus know they need a Christ-man friend in their lives. Christian men don't want failed jobs, marriages or estranged children. They are ripe for a win for their churches, communities, and our nation. They need men like us to depend on—to get in the game, persevere, and grow together in the knowledge of God and Christ-likeness.

You don't have to have a seminary degree or become a Bible scholar, have lived a perfect life or have all the answers. Were that true, none of us would qualify! That's why we all need Jesus. All we need now is a willing spirit to befriend another Christian man and grow together towards learning and applying deeper biblical truth in our lives.

> 66 Go therefore and make disciples of all nations, baptizing them in the name of the Father and of the Son and of the Holy Spirit. 99
> – Matthew 28:19

We simply lead men to the written Word of God and help them apply that written word of God within the varying seasons of their lives. No one ever spent time with God and remained the same! Over the course of the next year, change will happen in God's timing. All it takes is commitment, a willingness to invest into and grow together as followers of Jesus Christ.

> 66 Edmund Burke best revealed how Satan loves passivity: "The only thing necessary for the triumph of evil is for good men to do nothing." 99

Real-Life Discipleship

Section One

Spiritual Formation

Build the Relationship
Hebrews 3:13

Bible verses to reflect on when building a relationship:
1 Corinthians 13:4-7, 1 Peter 3:8, 1 Peter 4:8, 1 Thess. 5:11,
1 John 4:11-12

Things to center your time around:
Meet and get to know each other. Create small talk, and simply
learn about each other in great detail. You could spend weeks
just getting to know each other in a very real and intimate way.
Don't rush this process; discipleship is not a race.

Example questions:
Tell me about your dad.
Tell me about your wife.
Where did you grow up?
Tell me about your career.
Tell me about your children.
How long have you been married?

Notes from your time together:

Share Your Faith
1 Peter 3:15

Bible verses to reflect on when discussing your faith experience:
Romans 12:2, 2 Corinthians 3:18, 2 Corinthians 5:17, John 6:40, Romans 10:5-13, 1 John 1:9, John 14:6, Hebrews 11:6, 1 Peter 1:8, Ephesians 2:4-5,8

Things to center your time around:
Faith Commitment: when did Jesus become real for you? As the leader, begin by sharing your testimony and journey up to this point. It's important to clearly identify a faith commitment at some point, even if your follower hasn't grown much. If there is no clear faith commitment, then you need to share the gospel and introduce them to Christ. As the disciple-maker (leader), you need to model what a genuine and vibrant relationship with Jesus is and looks like.

Example questions:
Would you mind if I shared with you when I placed my faith in Christ?

Would you mind sharing with me when you placed your faith in Christ?

(It's ok if they don't have an answer for this question... that's why you are doing this. Encourage them and love them in this area and read through the scriptures referenced above.)

Does your wife or girlfriend have a genuine, vibrant relationship with Jesus Christ?

Notes from your time together:

Why We Are Here
Matthew 28:18-20 / 2 Timothy 2:2

Bible verses to reflect on when discussing where you are headed:
Proverbs 3:5-6, Romans 8:28, Ecclesiastes 3: 1-22, Jeremiah 1:5, Psalm 37:23

Things to center your time around:
Both of you should commit to meeting weekly for an extended period of time. We suggest committing to one year, 1-1.5 hours per week. In our experience, this relationship needs to be clearly spelled out. Don't leave room for confusion on what is happening during your time together. As the leader, you are strategically and intentionally getting to know each other to help grow the gospel in the followers life. Ensure expectations are communicated on both sides. Lay out where you are headed (if you choose to follow our guide) and see if there are areas that the follower would like to spend more time on then others.

Section One: Developing spiritual disciplines
Section Two: Examine the marriage relationship
Section Three: Examine the family, children and what does it mean to be the spiritual leader
Section Four: Discuss where the local church fits in with all this and a man's role in it
Section Five: Examine the career and how it is impacting their faith, family and church life
Section Six: Revisit your plans for growth in these areas
Section Seven: Develop a plan to multiply and impact more men

Example questions / statements:

What do you hope to get out of this?

Are you comfortable with where we are headed?

I hope to learn from you as you learn from what God has done in my life.

Do you understand Biblical discipleship? Can you explain your understanding?

Notes from your time together:

Developing Spiritual Disciplines
1 Timothy 4:7-8

Bible verses to reflect on when discussing where you are headed:
2 Timothy 2:15, 2 Timothy 3:16, 2 Timothy 4:2

Things to center your time around:

As the leader, discuss what it looks like to develop biblically rooted disciplines. Spiritual formation is the way to grow, and we must follow in the footsteps of Jesus Christ. Share with the follower ways that you have grown in Christ-likeness. Share with them what has worked for you and what has not. The point of developing spiritual disciplines is to drive men to God and His word, because that is where heart transformation happens—that leads to life change.

Remember: this should never be legalistic, but we do believe that doing things first out of duty for God can transform into a love and passion for obedience.

The Power of the 3 or P3

1. Understanding and reading the Bible with a **Plan** - Joshua 1:8
2. **Pray** with a purpose - 1 Thessalonians 5:16-18
3. **Purposely** align with godly men around you - Proverbs 11:14

Example questions:

What do you think would work for you?
Did you grow up around other godly people?
Do you have any regular spiritual disciplines?
Do you feel a desire to learn more about God?
Did you grow up reading the Bible and praying?

Notes from your time together:

Understanding and Reading
the Bible With a Plan
Joshua 1:8

Bible verses to reflect on when discussing where you are headed:
Joshua 3:9, Psalm 19:4, Matthew 4:4, John 1:1, John 1:14,
2 Timothy 3:15-16, Hebrews 4:12

Things to center your time around:
You can't use what you don't have, so the biggest step in discipling is developing a healthy biblical perspective. Properly
understanding the Bible and what we believe about it is very
important. As the leader, share ways that work to read the
Bible consistently and thoroughly. We must drive ourselves
and others to have an in-depth and intentional knowledge of
the entire Bible. Ask the follower how they study the Bible.
It's important to suggest some solid methods, but the point
is to lovingly encourage the follower to understand that
he needs to develop his own Bible study disciplines—not
from a legalistic perspective, but a genuine love for the word
of God because of the grace God has shown us (Romans

5:6-11). Part of your weekly meeting is accountability and understanding that developing spiritual disciplines is where growth takes place.

- **Observation** – What is going on in the text? What sticks out? What do you learn about God from the text? What do you learn about man from this text?

- **Interpretation** – What does the text mean? What is God saying/teaching in these verses? How should this text encourage you? Does the text warn you of anything?

- **Application** – How should I apply what I read to my life? Is their anything I should do in light of what I read? Is their anything I should repent of?

Example questions:
Do you regularly read and study the Bible?
Did your family grow up studying the Bible?
Why is what we believe about the Bible important?
Why do you think it's hard to read and study the Bible daily?
Would it add value to your life as a man, husband, and father if you were daily engaged in God's word?

Notes from your time together:

Pray With a Purpose
Matthew 26:41, Mark 1:35

Bible verses to reflect on when discussing where you are headed:
Luke 3:21-22, 1 Timothy 2:8, John 15:7, Philippians 4:6,
Mark 11:24, Romans 8:26, Matthew 6:6, Matt 6:9-13,
John 17, Romans 1:10

Things to center your time around:
God reveals Himself to people as we pray. As the leader, you
need the follower to understand that there is no right or
wrong, but there are some "Must Be's" in this area. How do
you have quiet time with God for personal reflection—time
to collect yourself and your thoughts? Take time to explain
that praying for their family and leading their wife and
children in daily prayer before the Lord has to take place.
The follower must understand leading in this area is his
responsibility... not his wife or children.

Example questions:
How do you pray?

When do you pray?
What do you pray about?
Do you use a prayer journal?
What does your prayer life look like?
Do you pray with your wife and children?
How do you think you could develop a stronger prayer life?

Notes from your time together:

Acknowledgments

WE WANT TO ATTEMPT TO MAKE some acknowledgments knowing we can't possibly name everyone we want to thank. If you are one of those people not listed but, know you had a part in our lives, to understand what it means to be more like Christ, Thank you!

We obviously must acknowledge Jesus Christ without His saving grace none of this is possible. Thank you for rescuing wretches like us! May we always make much more of you than of us!

We want to thank our wives, Jan Cheshire and Lisa Gensler. Behind every good man is an incredible woman. Thank you for loving us when we weren't lovable, for sticking with us in all the ups and downs of life and ministry. Most of all, thank you for your encouragement to stay the course and minister to the local church and her men.

Thank you to the following men who have made deep investments in our lives over the years. This book is many of our relationships being lived out in Real-life discipleship.

Scott Brindley
Jim Talley
Robert Lewis
Kenny Luck
Jerry Parks
Jeff Schulte
Vince D'Acchioli
Bob Bolin
Brian Doyle
Travis Bodden
Scott Payne

May we once and for all dispel the idea of a "self-made" man! That idea is as ridiculous as the scientist who calls out to God to tell Him that he can also create human life from dirt. To which God replies, "Get your own dirt!" Apart from God, it is impossible to do anything. May this book encourage you to invest in another man for the purpose of becoming more Christ-like, to the glory of God.

66 I am the vine; you are the branches.
Whoever abides in me and I in Him,
he it is that bears much fruit,
for apart from me you can do nothing. **99**

About the Authors

Tom Cheshire

Tom is married to his helper and wonderful wife, Jan Cheshire. Tom and Jan have two adult daughters Amelia and Lindleigh and son-in-law Logan. Tom served in the USMC 1976-1980 where he fell in love with aviation and a career in corporate aviation from 1980 until 2002. Tom has been in men's ministry really all his life but has been in leadership in both his church as an elder and in the community for the last 20 years.

Tom's passion for discipleship is born out of godly men investing in him to grow in Christ. Tom is also active in his church (Delta Church) as one of the Elders, with oversight of discipleship as one of his responsibilities. Tom has been an active member of the National Coalition of Men's Ministry (NCMM) since 2002, as well as one of the charter members of the national conference ministry, Iron Sharpens Iron (ISI). In 2007 Tom founded his second non-profit, Relevant Practical Ministry for Men (RPM) which is a servant ministry to the local church, to see her men maturing in Christ. RPM does that by investing in pastors and leaders to help them develop or strengthen a robust discipleship culture.

Tom Gensler

Tom and his beautiful wife Lisa have been married since 2004 and are in love with Jesus and each other. They have five children Ruby, Moses, Gabriel, Shiloh & Selah, and they reside in Decatur, IL.

Tom is a graduate from the University of Illinois in Springfield with a *Bachelor of Arts in Management*. He served six years as an Infantryman in the Illinois Army National Guard and spent 14 years working in the automotive industry gaining experience in every area of an auto dealership concluding with five years managing a multi-million-dollar service department with a multi-line dealership.

Tom has accumulated credit hours with *Lincoln Christian Seminary* and *Urbana Theological Seminary* in pursuit of a Masters of Divinity Degree.

He has also acquired an *Advanced Christian Life Coaching Certificate* and has completed a *Church Planting and Leadership Course* through *Dove Christian Fellowship International (DCFI).*

As a result of their own marriage struggles, the Gensler family is passionate about men understanding all that God intended for them, and in-turn loves seeing marriages and families thrive.

Tom & Lisa started volunteering with RPM in 2007 and joined the full-time staff as missionaries in Feb of 2013.